The *TILTABLE BOOK*

Turn the Tables on Your
Model Railroad

A How-To book by Ray Mathews

Second Edition

Cover Art and Illustrations by Ray Mathews

Raymond Mathews, Publisher

ISBN 978-0-9835790-0-7
Printed in the United States by Createspace

Disclaimer

The purpose of this manual is to educate the model hobbyist. The author has no liability or responsibility to persons using this manual with respect to loss or damage incurred, or alleged to have been incurred, directly or indirectly by the text instructions contained in this book.

The author can not guarantee the results obtained by any user of the *TILTABLE* technique of building model railroad tables; however, the author's experience with the *TILTABLE* concept has been excellent, the construction technique has saved time, is easier than other methods identified, and the author was able to manage the normal population functions of adding wiring and mounting scenery with less work, and no crawling under and reaching over the model railroad tables in the process of building.

READY TO BUILD BENCHWORK for your railroad, but afraid you'll spend *hours* on your back *under* the table wiring with a hot soldering iron, or stretching *over* the table, sawing, drilling, painting, and gluing your knockout scenery?

ARE YOU INVOLVED WITH NTRAK? Do you *move* your module to a work bench for wiring or crawl *over* and *under* the table for scenery work? Do you *store* or *move* your railroad from place to place at times?

Wouldn't you like an easier way?

If the answer to that question is '*YES*', then *TILTABLE* is for you!

This book is about *TILTABLE*, the railroad benchwork that *tilts so you can sit in a comfortable chair and work on the top or bottom of your table as no one has ever been able to do before.*

No more back aches, sore muscles, sawdust in your eyes, or solder on your clothes and skin.

No more balancing acts while working on your scenery, afraid your arm will drag across that trestle or building and create a manmade tornado.

Here is a benchwork technique that makes the work easier – **and your hobby more fun!**

In this book you'll see complete **How-To** instructions on each phase of building with over 100 illustrations and photographs, and tips to aid you in building.

TILTABLE gives you *storage* options, *moving* options, makes module *joining* as easy as **NTrak,** and provides you with a strong, permanent benchwork that works on *single* tables, *room-encompassing* railroads as well as *cantilevered* and *shelf* railroads, *foldaways,* and, yes, *NTRAK* modules.

And for you adventurous modelers who appreciate an *extra bonus*, there's a **Surprise** at the end called **DIAL-A-PIKE.**

In 1991 Ray Mathews decided to build another room-sized railroad layout; however, he didn't like to lie on his back to work on wiring, or reach over the table to work on scenery. Ray treated this like any other engineering problem he'd tackled in the past, and *Voila! The TILTABLE was born.*

TILTABLE works because it's logical. It works for inexperienced modelers, mature modelers, and yes, even those in *wheelchairs* who have hand and arm control.

For every owner of *The TILTABLE Book*, the rewards are many.

Join the *NEW AGE* of railroad benchwork called…

TILTABLE!

The *TILTABLE* Book

Table of Contents

Chapter 1

WHICH RAILROAD FOR YOU?

This book is about *TILTABLE*, a technique of building that was developed to save you time and work and put the *FUN* back in your building by getting you out from *under* your railroad tables and by letting you relax in a chair while working on the top scenery or the bottom wiring.

But you have to do your part, too.

You have to use your imagination to see how to *apply TILTABLE* principles to your own layouts – just like you would do with any other benchwork you build.

You'll see examples of how to do this in **Chapter 2**

To start you off on the path to more pleasurable benchwork, think about your railroad layout from various aspects.

The first thing you must decide on is the *type* of railroad you're going to build. Just what *kind* of railroad do you have in mind?

- A benchwork railroad located at the periphery of a room?
- A cantilevered railroad set high on the wall - maybe even running from room to room?
- A foldaway or rollaway railroad that's stored when not in use?
- An **NTrak** module that can be taken from place to place?
- A railroad table accessible for those in wheelchairs?

There's usually a good reason for building a specific type of benchwork for your railroad; for instance:

• *Joe's son wants a railroad, but mom wants it put away when he's finished playing with it - and a foldaway or a rollaway evolves.*

• *25-year-old Tim loves trains, but a regular free-standing train table doesn't fit with his apartment's modern decor - a unique shelf railroad evolved, mounted high on the wall and running from room to room around the periphery - out of the way of little or big hands, and an absolutely great conversation piece.*

• *Jack, however, has a full basement, (he's the envy of most of us), and he plans and builds a forty-foot long table along the walls, and even has room to double back into the center - if he can get his wife to relinquish her hold on that center territory.*

Over the years, railroad hobby magazines have published numerous articles and illustrations covering all manner of railroad layouts, and they've discussed benchwork construction methods, like butt-joint and L-girder – which are used in the *TilTable* benchwork technique to make your scenery and wiring work easier than ever before!

You'll be shown how to build *TilTables* for a room, a single table, a store-away, cantilevered, shelf, and even **NTrak** modules.

Once you have a layout plan developed, the next step in building a model railroad is to construct the benchwork on which track and scenery can be built, right? Well, yes, but don't start cutting chips until you've considered the next three chapters.

For the more experienced model railroaders, you may want to browse through these chapters just to be certain there's nothing new that you haven't seen before.

The real *building* starts in **Chapter 5.**

To the **newer model railroader**, these first few chapters are directed at you.

For instance, in **Chapter 2**, you'll read about things you should consider when you're getting *ready* to build. These issues relate to any type of benchwork construction, but you'll be shown how they apply particularly to *TilTable* construction.

You'll read all about **aisle widths**, **table viewing height**, **table length**, **free-form table edges**, your railroad's **scale**, your **available space**, and others. You'll even read a word or two about **tools** and **materials**.

You'll read a good deal in this book about *portability* since so much model railroading today is done in a *modular* fashion so that railroad benchwork can be *moved* easily from place to place - and even *joined* to other railroads.

In **Chapter 3**, you'll get a rundown on the *types* of benchwork you can build, with useful illustrations to help you understand the construction. You'll see why L-girder construction is favored, but you'll be shown a T-girder technique which is an alternative to L-girders and is just as effective plus has its advantages, too.

In **Chapter 4** you'll learn all about the *TilTable* concept and how to *use* it, and in **Chapter 5,** you'll be shown how to *build* a *TilTable*.

Chapter 6 shows you how to build *cantilevered* and *shelf* benchwork with explanations and illustrations of the 'standard' techniques, and then how to build a cantilevered *TilTable*. You'll find that a tilting table has advantages as a cantilevered table.

Chapter 7 shows how to build an *NTrak module* using *TilTable*, and even shows a *'nesting'* technique for two modules.

Tricky benchwork situations are addressed in Chapters 8 and 9, and is, well …

A Step Beyond...

Chapter 2

BEFORE YOU BUILD...

Let's take a look at what you should consider before you build anything.

Tools to *Consider* (**See** *Photo*)

Tools used in building model railroad benchwork.

Tools used for benchwork   Drywall screws used   Screw pilot for many holes

We live in the age of power tools. The author utilizes several power tools, and recommends you consider them in your own building, since they can be used in home repairs and other projects, too. Some useful tools are:

Circle Saw - great for cutting girders and joists to length and trimming plywood sheets to size.

Jigsaw or Scroller saw - This is an all-around useful tool for cutting irregular shapes and is highly recommended for ribbon roadbeds.

Power Drill - A time saver when you're fastening lots of screws or making holes for pivot bolts. A drill combined with a screw pilot will save time and prepare your screw holes for joining. You can put a sanding disk on the drill, too.

Drill Bits - **A set** of **wood bores bits** are useful on model railroads and are great for home projects, too.

Metal bits are useful, **too,** where you have small holes to drill in metal parts.

Power Screwdriver - **If** you're contemplating a multi-table railroad, get this! It will save time and sore wrists. It can screw screws in or out. Be sure to get one with good torque. These are not as popular as they once were, but they're lighter in weight than your portable drill and not as hard on the arms when used constantly.

Clamps - A must on a model railroad, especially when you're initially building pedestals, and table frames. You can get them in sets of three. It's nice to have several sizes, but the author uses a 3/4-inch jaw frequently.

Sanding Block - Useful for removing burrs and smoothing surfaces. You can get to places you can't reach with a power sander. It's a good idea to have about three grades of sandpaper on hand; coarse, medium, and fine.

Safety Aids - You should consider **Safety glasses a** MUST in any tool operation. Ear Protectors are worthwhile when using power drills, circle saws, and other loud power tools.

A Dust Mask is good to use when sanding, sawing, or spraying.

Many other tools are available like radial arm saws, table saws, etc., but most of these require that you take the work to *them*. If you have these tools, they can be useful, but they are not a necessity in model railroad table building.

Wood - You'll only need a few types of wood for table building.

Plywood - 1/8- to 1/2-inch.

Useful as a table top, as roadbed ribbon, as corner gussets, etc.

Pine, Spruce, or Fir

Depending on where you live, these woods are readily available in 2x2 for legs or pedestal posts, I xl, 1x2, lx3, and 1x4 for girders and joists in lengths of 8, 12, and 16 feet.

You can save money by buying longer lengths and cutting them to length yourself, but you may not be able to handle them with an automobile.A car-top carrier with cross yokes and strap will hold the wood down tightly - plywood sheets, too.

Screws (See Photo) – Check out #6x1-l/4-inch flathead drywall screws; these work successfully for most table work. They're less expensive than the #8 flathead screw usually recommended for model tables. Also they have great gripping strength due to their rough finish. They come in boxes of 100 for convenience.

Screw Pilot (See Photo)

Whatever size screw you decide on for your table work, invest in a screw pilot to pre-drill the screw holes. It will make your work go much faster, A good screw pilot that is 1/4-inch *shorter* than the screw is perfect. That way the tip of the screw bites into the wood at the end, giving the screw more gripping strength.

Now let's talk about *your railroad table* a minute. There are many considerations that may help you zero in on the 'right' type of railroad table. Considering these things now might help you choose the 'best' benchwork at the beginning and avoid having to redo it later - or worse still, build a construction that boxes you in or limits your operating possibilities.

SIZE *of Your Pike* - small, *Medium, or LARGE?*

Size of a railroad is relative. Some model railroaders are never satisfied with the

4

size and scope of their creations, and continue to plan and expand to new dimensions every year.

> ### Scales used in many plan books
> **N-scale = 1/2", TT-scale = 3/4", HO-scale = 1", S-scale = 1-1/2", O-scale = 2"**

You can put a mainline, industry spur, small siding or yard, a bridge, a tunnel, and many other features on a *coffee table,* so size isn't really necessary. But if you like to see trains run on and on ... and on, then length of track - and probably size - is important to you.

Expert model railroaders say to "start small". The author's first pike was an HO oval on the living room floor. Next was a 3x5-foot HO multi-level railroad, built using 1-depth construction (sometimes called 'butt-joint') on casters in the Living room of a 3-room apartment. My wife tolerated the sawdust and other mess.

For lack of any serious definition, let's classify railroad layout size as follows:

SMALL - Under 16 square feet in area; that about 4x4-feet square.

This includes suitcase, coffee table, foldaway, roll-under or rollaway, elevated or raised by pulley in a garage, for instance, and includes table sizes such as 2x4, 4x4, 2x8, etc. Also included are **NTrak** modules - usually 2 by 4-, 6-, or 8- feet. We'll discuss **NTrak** railroading in detail in **Chapter 7.**

MEDIUM - 16 to 32 square feet in area.

This includes 4x8, 4x5, and 3x11 sizes and could be multiple **NTrak** modules as well: two 2x4, two 2x6, or two 2x8, or any combination of these.

LARGE - Greater than 32 square feet.

This includes the room-filling kind which may have tables so wide that lift-out hatches are required in the center of tables in order to work on track and scenery, or a "snake" benchwork of tables with aisles on one or both sides of the table for access, This benchwork may be in the form of alphabet characters like an "O", "C", "J", "H", etc. You'll see later how *TilTable benchwork can work well even with O- and S-gage railroad tables, and in many cases eliminate the need for center hatches.*

Also classed as large are the multi-shelf or "double-decker" layouts with cantilevered tables and shelves above or below the main table level. This allows for lots of track and rolling stock, and spacious storage facilities.

Whatever size is chosen, remember that in general, size can be equated to cost, maintenance time, building time, storage needs, and space availability. If you try for too much at the start, you may get discouraged and lose interest. Your railroad may never get to an operating stage.

This is why smart model railroaders say to 'start small'. That way you get experience in all phases of railroading before you move onto something large and complex. By living with your smaller pike for a while, you'll soon generate a list of features you'd like to incorporate into a new pike - or you actually build some of them into your existing pike.

Another approach available to all is the **model railroad club**, where you can meet modelers of similar persuasion, learn from the 'experts', run trains, build rolling stock and structures, build scenery for the club, and learn how to buy, sell, and trade railroad equipment. From specialized railroad hobby magazines, you can find out where model railroad events will be held and about model railroad clubs, too.

Train Table Width and Length (See Fig. 2-1)

Once you've established a track layout plan, you can see quickly how wide your table is at any point. The same applies to the table length. With continuous benchwork, once built, the entire layout takes considerable work in order to make changes or modifications.

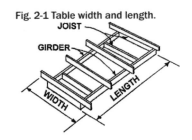

Fig. 2-1 Table width and length.

With a modular approach, each section can be altered by itself with less impact on adjacent sections.

Conversely, the sectioned layout will require more initial work to build -- wiring table-to-table, for instance. The table width can be played off against aisle width to get the best overall combination in each part of the railroad layout.

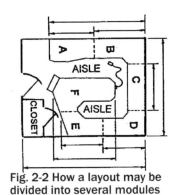

Fig. 2-2 How a layout may be divided into several modules

Fixed or Movable Layout

The average American moves once every five years - or stated another way, 20% of the population moves *every year!* That's 50 million people and many of those are model railroaders.

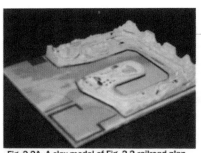

Fig. 2-2A A clay model of Fig. 2-2 railroad plan.

More than likely, the average model railroader builds or moves his railroad, too. It's this mobility in railroad building that makes *portability* attractive. Building a railroad in pieces that are easily handled makes it easier to upgrade or dispose of it. Storage is easier, and transporting tables from place to place is simpler.

So remember, that if you have ideas for a large railroad, cut it down to size by dividing it into manageable modules. Then you can work on each module as if it were a railroad by itself. **(See Fig. 2-2 and Photo, Fig. 2-2A as an example of a sectioned railroad)**

Available Space

You may be the modeler who has to store his layout after each use. You'll see ideas for storing and sharing space as you go through the book. Or maybe you have a room, an attic space, a corner, or a wall. The availability of space may very well dictate the kind of pike you build - and the *kind* of benchwork you put under it.

For example, if you have only an 8-foot wall in your family room available to you, and can only build into the room 3 feet, you're not only limited as to how much track you can put in that length, but what *scale* will allow you to build a *return loop* to turn your trains around. In N-scale, that 36-inch width will allow broad curve radii of 15 inches or more, but you can't *build* a turning loop in 0- scale or S-scale, and in HO, this width would limit you to sharp curves only. **(See Fig. 2-3)**

The Scale You'll Use

As mentioned, the scale you model in has a major effect on the benchwork. It dictates how wide the table top has to be (when you're building return loops, for instance). With larger scales like 0-scale and very wide railroads, access hatches have to be planned into the layout just to get to the table center for track and scenery purposes. I'll show you how you can build wide 0-scale tables as easily as N-scale - and maybe without hatches at all!

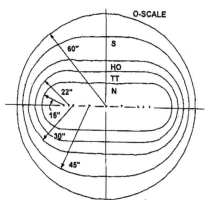

Fig. 2-3 Comparison of curve radii.

As can be seen from the **Curve radii** illustration, providing a turning loop of track requires a lot of real estate especially in the larger scales like 0-scale. This tremendous real estate requirement is one of the reasons many developed plans shown in model railroad track plan books are 'point-to-point' rather than 'loop-to-loop'; plans without loops take much less table width. Also, of course, they're more like real railroads which generally don't have turning loops. So unless you have a rather large space available, you might be forced to limit your layout to point-to-point with large scales like 0-scale, plan a loop-to-loop arrangement with a smaller scale like HO or N-scale, or consider a multiple shelf arrangement which can run in an oval.

Table Height for Best Viewing (See Fig. 2-4)

Taking the advice of expert model railroaders, a good table height for viewing is a 42-44-inch height to the top of your rolling stock at zero elevation.

This gives you the ability to:
- View your railroad from a sitting position
- Reach over the table
- Work under the table
- Duck under the table
- Store or move your railroad table

Fig. 2-4 Viewing height.

If you must have folding legs or room to store things under your railroad, the height is important, and should be decided early, although you can change the table height later if necessary. Also consider the 'duck- under' aspect built into some railroads. Duck-under refers to a railroad where you must duck-under to get into the center of the pike, or duck-under to get to some part of it. In the past, if it was high enough to duck under, it was too high to lay track or build scenery unless you stood on a ladder, box, or bench. A modeler friend told me that he sets the table height by sitting on the floor with his head up. All joists and girders must be above his head. Actually, his table height is about 44 inches.

You'll see that the *TilTable* technique is perfect for your desired table height because there *IS* no under-the-table work.

Aisle Widths Around Your Railroad (See Fig. 2-5)

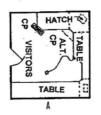  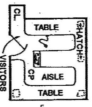 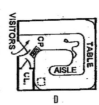

Fig. 2-5 Examples of aisle-way planning on large railroads, showing visitor areas, control panel locations, and walk-around control locations.

Whatever size and shape your railroad takes, you have to have *access* to all parts of it, and that means aisle ways or access panels. It's best to plan for aisles right at the beginning when you develop a track plan, because you'll have uncomfortable moments and impossible situations without good aisles. A good rule of thumb is to allow about 24 -30", but wider where persons will be passing one another. On many home layouts that width takes too much track room away from the railroad. You can get by with aisles as narrow as 18, but this is a bare minimum if you must work on scenery, track, or wiring from that aisle way width.

Here again, you'll see that *TilTable* benchwork eliminates this problem and allows you to work comfortably without much aisle space. **(See Fig. 2-6)** Aisles are even more important if you are considering walk-around controls on the layout.

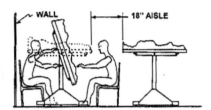

Fig. 2-6 TilTable allows ready access and ease of work on tables even with narrow aisles

Control Panel & Walk-Around Control Location

Once you zero in on a track plan you like, you must consider the best location for your **control panel**. You want to put it where you can view most, or all, of your railroad layout in one sweep, be out of the way of other railroaders walking around with train controls, and still have room to move about for switching and, perhaps, cab control.

Walk-around controls should be placed at strategic points, preferably where little or no interference with other railroaders will occur.

Visitor Viewing Area

Since visitors tend to congregate where the action is - around the control panel - this is a good place to plan for some extra space so that visitors can watch the action and not be in your way, where you and they can talk without distracting everyone else, and where they can see some of your interesting scenery without straining.

Health - Your Physical Condition

Model railroading has always had a core of mature hobbyists. Crawling over and under model railroad tables is no one's idea of fun, but to get in on the fun, modelers of all ages have had to accept the bending, stooping, head-bumping, and the rest in order to enjoy the hobby. With *TilTable* construction, modelers can *enjoy* model railroading again, and work in comfort while wiring, laying track, or pasting up scenery.

After Your Table is Built -- Yes, the chapter title suggests what you should consider and do *before* your table is built, but it's necessary to put this *up front* so that you will *consider* these things as you're *buildmg* your table.

Sometimes a girder or joist is directly under a turnout or switch solenoid. *Bad news!* A little forethought could prevent much rework.

So let's look quickly at what you're going to do with this table **AFTER** you build it. **(See Fig. 2-7)**

Soon after your base table is built, you will want to start adding support for your track. There are several favored techniques for the track support, depending on how much effort you intend to put into topography. These include:

Flat Plain (See Fig 2-7A)

You can simply attach a piece of 1/4-inch plywood to the table top and lay roadbed (usually cork) right on the plywood and then lay your track. But even in this simple arrangement, *be warned.*

If you have turnouts and switch solenoids in your track plan, be sure to lay out your plan to scale to find out where to put joists - and even outside girders in some cases - so that they aren't directly under turnouts and solenoids.

Paper Dolls, Cookie Cutter, or Cutaways (See Fig 2-7B)

Here you may cut away from the plywood sheet the ribbon representing the supporting terrain (the sub-roadbed) under your track. This ribbon can then be raised or lowered as desired to provide uneven topography to challenge your trains and give your countryside a more realistic appearance.

Loose Ribbon, Pasta Strip, riser presents an easily-solved plaster,

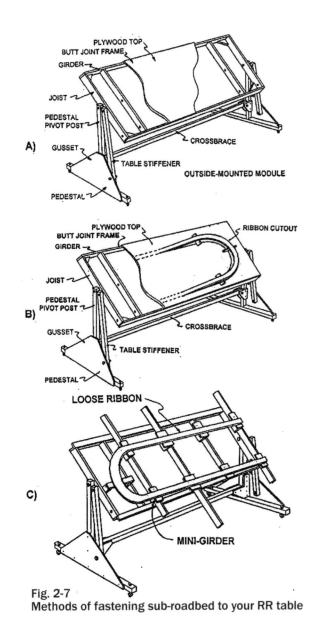

Fig. 2-7
Methods of fastening sub-roadbed to your RR table

plywood, Styrofoam, or other Spaghetti, Snake, etc. (See Fig 2-7C)

In this technique you probably don't have a plywood sheet on your table. Instead you cut out the ribbons and support them at various elevations - determined from your track plan - around your table, Several materials have been used successfully for these ribbons: Homasote, plywood, and even 'splines' which are composites of thinner wood strips set vertically and combined to produce a sub roadbed which can be curved as needed and is extremely solid.

Except for the Flat topography, your sub-roadbed will need to be supported throughout your layout to give it rigidity at the various elevations required. The supports used - called *risers, elevators,* etc. - can be sturdily fastened to the joist with dry-wall screws.

Attaching the sub roadbed to the riser presents an easily-solved problem. Since cork roadbed and track will soon cover the sub roadbed or ribbon, attaching the ribbon with screws from the top is risky. At some later time you may need to separate the ribbon from the **riser**.

Now you'll have to remove **track** and **cork roadbed** and...

Wait a minute? We said this is an easily-solved problem - and it *IS!*

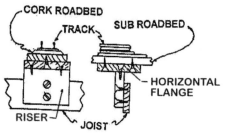

Fig. 2-8 A mini-girder under your sub-roadbed will allow you to raise it to any desired height.

By adding a **horizontal flange** on *top* of the **riser**, you create a mini-girder, either a T- or L-girder. Now you can screw up through the flange from below into the ribbon. I recommend you screw the *flange* to the *riser* from the *top* - just like you do when you create a T- or L-girder. That way you aren't working with narrow pieces of wood that may split when you begin screwing into them.

Adding Scenery Base Material (See Photo)

After your sub-roadbed, roadbed, and track are in place, you can fill in the hills and valleys with the scenery base. This can be 'papier mache', plaster, plywood, Styrofoam, or other materials which are easily molded or shaped.

In recent years good results have been achieved with Styrofoam sheets which you can get in thicknesses of 1, 2, 3, and 4 inches as insulation - usually pale blue in color.

You can saw it, file it with a rasp, drill it, glue it, paint it, and easily change it later if you want. Also, Styrofoam is super lightweight which makes your table easier to move. You have to be careful not to damage it - but that's true of ANY scenery base.

A view of a scenery-populated TilTable.

Once the scenery base is in place, you can either coat it with plaster, or simply spray-glue the Styrofoam with sand and lichen and color it with various sprays or paint it with a brush where necessary. Good results have been achieved with the latter - and besides, it's a lot less work than adding plaster.

A word of caution. Some glues attack Styrofoam and 'melt' it. The author used Elmer's Wood Glue successfully. There are probably other glues that work, too.

Shown is a *TilTable* module with finished scenery and lots of blue Styrofoam in those thar' hills and valleys. You'll see more views of this module later. This is Table-A of the room plan of Fig. 2-2.

Chapter 3

BENCHWORK TYPES

The generally-accepted railroad table building methods have been given the labels **'butt-joint'** and **'L-girder'** construction. Let's look briefly at each so you'll recognize them.

Butt-Joint Construction (See Fig. 3-1)

Here you simply build a a rectangular frame, insert table joists, mount the frame on four legs, and start populating the frame with risers, sub roadbed, track, wire, and scenery. With butt-joint construction, you end up with one-depth of wood, i.e., 3-inches of a 1x3, and everything is built over, under, and through this framework. To hold the joists together, you need a front and rear face board - which are really vertical girders.

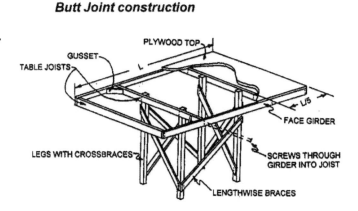

L-Girder Construction (See Figs 3-2A)

This benchwork type was developed in the I 970's by the late Linn Westcott, who is considered a pathfinder by most of us.

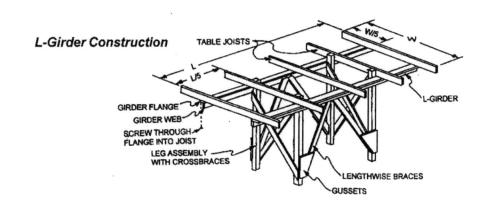

Here the girders are attached to the four legs, and table joists are added on top of them, allowing a free-form flow of the table edges. This free-form character can give the railroad a more realistic look since the edges aren't necessarily square-cornered or straight-edged; however, free form table edges can be a lot of work, and the majority of modelers simply don't want to expend the time for them.

With L-girder construction, you have *two* depths of wood - a girder depth and a table joist depth above. Again, everything is built over, under, and through this framework of girders and joists.

Many railroaders build L-girder benchwork because of its slightly better strength, coupled with the free-form edges, and the *added* plus that you can screw all joists to the girders from underneath though the girder flanges.

This is important when you have to crawl under the table - but you won't have to do that with *TilTable* construction.

Note: (See Fig. 3-2B)

A 'T'-girder has basically the same load-carrying capabilities as an L-girder; however, making a T-girder has several advantages:

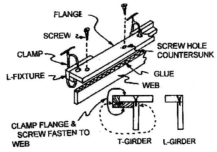

Fig. 3-2B A "T"-girder has about the same load-bearing strength as an L-girder – with other advantages, too.

• You can screw up into the flange from either side of the vertical web of the girder.
• The vertical (web) and horizontal (flange) can have the same widths, making your materials handling easier.
• There is no front or rear to the T-girder.
• The added weight for two T-girders versus two L-girders is about 5.5 oz. per linear foot of girder length, so a 6-foot table weighs about 2 lb. more than an L-girder, an increase in frame weight of about 10%.

It's your choice.

Just remember throughout the book that a T-girder could be used wherever an L-girder is used. Note the L-fixture used when assembling the T-girder. Use two of these, one at each girder end. **(See Fig. 3-2B)**

Cantilever Construction
(See *Figs. 3-3 and 3-4*)

The basic cantilever consists of three pieces that form a triangle (the strongest of all building elements): a 2x2 vertical called a **pilaster**, a diagonal 2x2 called a **brace**, and a horizontal table support **arm** or **bracket arm**.

A cantilever can use butt-joint or L-girder benchwork, too. In *this* method, the table top is usually *fastened* to the wall around the periphery of the room.

For a '*permanent*' railroad, the cantilever method is an ideal support. Leveling is more critical in the initial stages of construction since, once fastened to a wall, it is difficult to reposition.

Since you don't have legs at all corners, less lumber is used in this benchwork, and because the table is a *ledge*, there is ample room underneath for cleaning, working on wiring, and storage. Of course, you must add a diagonal brace between the base of the wall and the front of the table. All load-bearing is taken through this diagonal and transmitted to the lower wall anchor which, as shown in the moment diagram, acts as a fixed pivot for the entire assembly to rotate about. All construction methods; butt-joint, L-girder, and, yes,

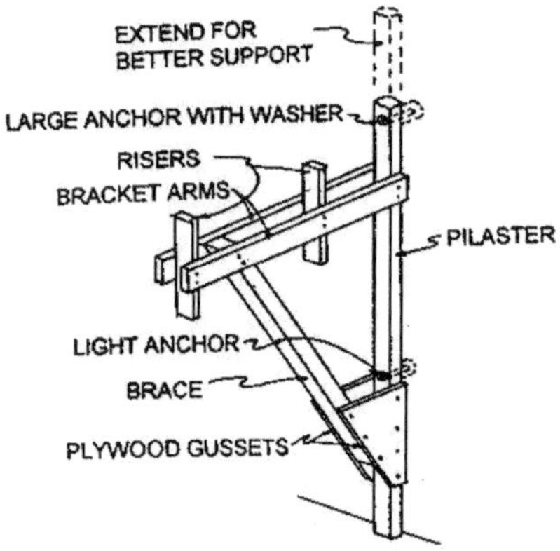

Fig. 3-3 Components of a cantilevered benchwork.

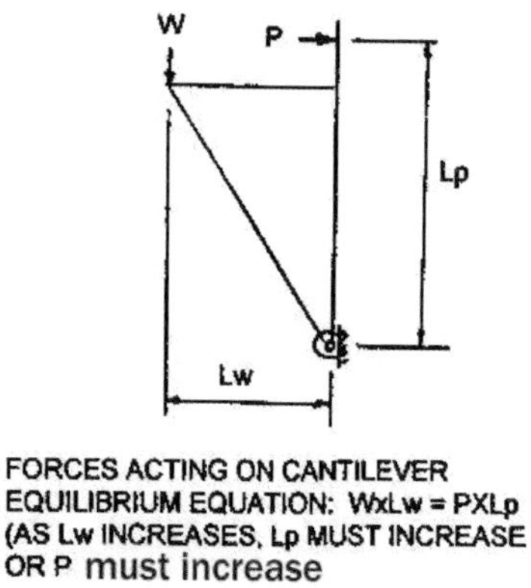

EXTEND FOR BETTER SUPPORT

LARGE ANCHOR WITH WASHER

RISERS

BRACKET ARMS

PILASTER

LIGHT ANCHOR

BRACE

PLYWOOD GUSSETS

FORCES ACTING ON CANTILEVER EQUILIBRIUM EQUATION: WxLw = PxLp (AS Lw INCREASES, Lp MUST INCREASE OR P must increase

Fig. 3-4 Forces acting on a cantilevered frame.

TilTable, too, can be used in the cantilever scheme. If you believe that you will ever move this assembly, be sure to consider construction methods that will allow the table to be removed easily.

The pilaster can be fastened to the wall stud at top and bottom with lag bolts, the top bolt being most important for load-bearing, since the weight of the table will attempt to pull the pilaster away from the wall, With this in mind, the higher you can fasten this anchor bolt, the more load the structure can support.

If the table width becomes *too* wide, and the diagonal forms an included angle with the pilaster of more than 45 degrees, you may want to consider an *outer* leg. Now you're back to a 'legged' table again. As you can see, there are table width limits to cantilevered railroads, too.

Distance between cantilevers should be such that no sag in the table girders occurs. This depends somewhat on the type of girder used and the table length. Thus, on top of the table base, a butt-joint frame or L-girder frame can be mounted - or the diagonal can be fastened directly to the girder joist as in *TilTable* construction.

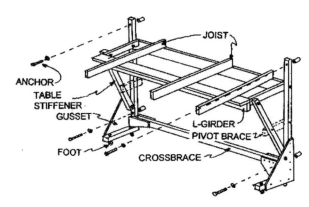

Fig. 3-5 TilTable as a cantilevered railroad table.

If the presence of a table leg or 'foot' is not objectionable, the *TilTable* construction method can be used here to great advantage. (**See Fig. 3-5**)

Thus in the early stages of building, the table can be tilted up or down so that track work, wiring, and scenery can be added much more comfortably without the need to work over or under the cantilevered table. Once populated, the 'half-pedestal' can be moved against the wall and fastened to the wall the same as any cantilever would be. An alternative to this is to simply eliminate the pedestal '**foot**', and attach the half- pedestal or cantilever to the wall with the **pilaster** or pedestal. It should be mentioned that if you're thinking *of joining* two or more modules in a cantilever arrangement, remember that *outside-mounting* probably shouldn't be considered since pilasters are generally fixed to the wall. You might want to build the half pedestal *TilTable* mentioned, populate the table with wiring and scenery, and mount it to the wall supports so that the table is *inside-mounted*. That way you still have *Tilt* capability, but can join all modules.

A **shelf** is simply a *cantilever* at a higher elevation. There are at least three ways to

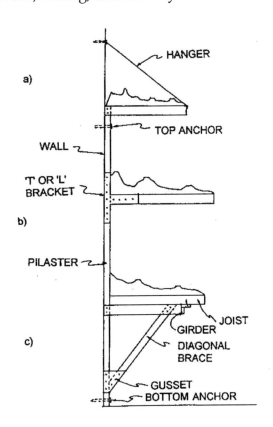

Fig. 3-6 Methods of supporting a cantilevered railroad shelf.

support a cantilever: **(See Fig. 3-6)**

a) *Hang the shelf from a support* - the support can be a wooden arm, a chain, or even a very thin, strong wire. The problem is that the hanging support is generally in the way of tracks or scenery and detracts from the overall appearance.

b) Support the shelf with a T-bracket or L-bracket, fastened to both the pilaster and the support arm of the shelf.

c) Support the shelf with a diagonal brace as described in the cantilever scheme above. Metal brackets are rather expensive, and a quantity of these are necessary if a long railroad is to be built at the periphery of a room.

Another technique is to use a tall pilaster - almost floor to ceiling - and *construct a half-pedestal TilTable* including a lower table and an upper shelf. **(See Fig. 3-7)**

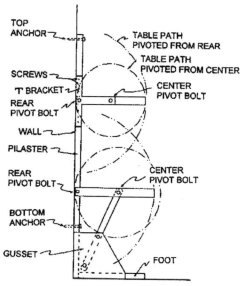

Fig. 3-7 A floor-to-ceiling pilaster will hold an upper and lower cantilevered table.

In this case, adjustable feet are not required, as the height of the table will be fixed by wall and floor. The upper table can be supported by a "T-bracket", but instead of *screws* in the joist, two **bolts** can be used as shown. This gives you *two* alternatives for tilting the table in order to work:

a) a *rear* bolt pivot allows pivoting the table up and down about 90-degrees;

b) a *center* bolt pivot of the joist allows the table to be rotated a full 360-degrees (barring high scenery, of course), if outside mounted, and about 85-degrees if inside mounted.

In a similar fashion, two bolts can be added to the bottom table. The gusset is configured a bit differently so that a bolt or screws can be added to support the diagonal brace. In this manner, the bottom table can also be rotated around the *rear* bolt by pulling the center bolt, or around the *center* bolt by pulling the rear bolt. Pivoting about the rear bolt also allows

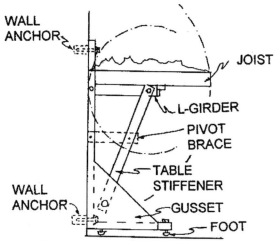

Fig. 3-8 A half-TilTable is built, then anchored to the wall, and the foot is removed, if desired.

the table to be stored close to the wall in a vertical position. **(See Fig. 3-8)**

Once anchored to the wall top and bottom, the foot can be removed, if desired, for better clearance under the table.

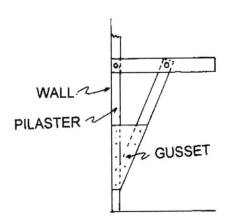

Fig. 3-9 An alternate arrangement with a gusset

One more tilt arrangement is possible, and that's to pivot the table top around the outside of the table, requiring you to extend or replace the diagonal with a longer arm.

Shown in **Fig. 3-9** is an alternative arrangement without the foot, but with a gusset supporting the diagonal brace so that the table can be pivoted.

If the vertical space between the table and the shelf is slightly greater than the longer width of table or shelf, then both the table and shelf can be tilted up and down for easier working on top and bottom. Note that if done correctly the pilaster can be fastened to the wall, and tilt of both table and shelf can still be done.

Comparison of Butt-Joint and L-girder Construction

Since butt-joint and L-girder construction are used in all forms of benchwork, let's compare them:

Table removal

Since both framing methods are attached securely to the legs, removal of the table top is rare. Of the two methods, butt-joint frames could be removed more easily.

With L-girders, *there are no corner gussets* to hold or maintain 90-degrees in the table frame, so scenery would have to provide stiffness if the table is removed (rather risky). It's a good idea to *add* these corner gussets - just in case. I'll discuss this later when showing the details of building benchwork. **(See Fig. 3-10)**

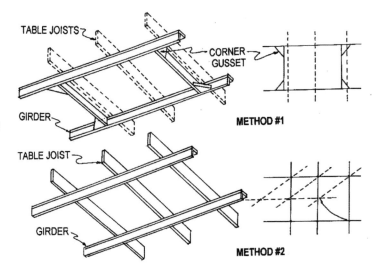

Fig 3-10 The advantages of using corner gussets in benchwork.

Assembly

The L-girder (or T-girder) is made of *two* pieces of wood at right angles, so there is more work involved. *The* L-girder takes the place of the front and rear face *girder* of the butt-joint frame. If analyzed, it's obvious that inner table joists can be placed as desired in *either* method with some planning, but you have a bit more freedom with L-girder. Also, legs, can be placed in the most strategic position to support either frame, so load bearing isn't so different end-to-end.

Space under the table

Butt-joint wins when comparing both schemes with the same table joist height above the floor since it's 1-*depth* whereas L-girder is 2-*depth:* however, we're talking **about a** 3 to 4 inch difference in storage height - rather slight.

Bending strength

L-girder benchwork has slightly better load-bearing strength due to the girder cross-section. With butt-joint benchwork, the load is carried in shear through the screws holding the joists to the face girder. In L-girder, the full weight of the table bears on top of the girders themselves, but it can be argued that the load is carried in shear through the screws holding the girder to the legs. In reality, bending strength only becomes a factor in *long* tables in terms of table *sag, and only if you have some very heavy scenery on your table.*

Table edges

L-girder construction allows a pleasant free-form edge because table joists are on top of the girders instead of in-line with them as in butt-joint construction.

You can extend the edge of a butt-joint table in a free-form fashion, too, by extending 1/2- or 3/4-inch plywood beyond the joist edge somewhat without support. You may have to add supports under the plywood in order to attach aisle boards to the table.

Be careful if you decide to *notch* joists or girders. A sharp notch in a board reduces its strength greatly and makes a break due to impact a distinct possibility.
(See Fig. 3-11)

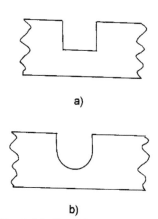

a)

b)

Fig. 3-11 Notching a joist or girder:
a) Sharp corners will break easier.
b) Round corners have better impact strength.

If you must notch a board, put a radius at the bottom of the notch as shown. This will eliminate the sharp corners.

- Assembly appears to be easier with butt-joint.
- L-girder allows free-form table edges.
- L-girder has slightly better strength in long tables.

Fig. 3-13 Crawling Under the table is not fun...

Fig. 3-14 Reaching over the layout can cause harm to your scenery.

- When tables are *against* walls, fastening table joists is easier from underneath with L-girder.

Sorry, Mr. Railroad builder!
With these generally-used benchwork methods comes a bevy of *other* problems such as **(See Figs. 3-13 and 3-14):**

- You must crawl **under** the table for wiring and positioning, drilling holes, fastening risers, soldering, and sawing – oh, my.
- You must **reach over** your track work and scenery to work on your railroad.
- You may bump your head, drip solder on yourself, get sawdust in your eyes and on your clothes while drilling or sawing *under* the table.

Table joist fastening (See Fig. 3-12)

As mentioned, L-girder construction has the advantage of under-the- table fastening through the girder flange, while in butt-joint, joists are fastened to the *sides* of the front and rear face girders; however, you still have to crawl under the table to fasten girders.

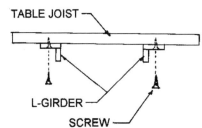

Fig. 3-12 Joists can be attached to T- or L-girders with screws driven from the bottom.

Butt-joint vs L-girder Conclusions:

- The butt-joint table can be removed more easily from the legs.
- The butt-joint table has more room underneath.

You may snag your delicate scenery while working on *top* of the table.

You may discover sore muscles from *bending, stooping, reaching, squatting, and crawling.*

Most of your wiring will be done *flat on your back* on a mechanic's creeper - or worse – scooting on your back on the floor.

If you're not satisfied with this situation, then you're ready for Chapter 4...

Butt Joint construction

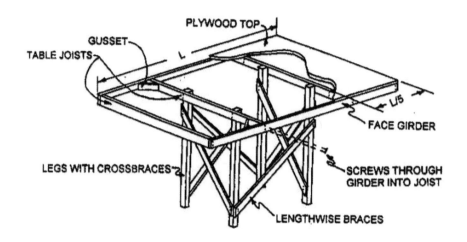

L-Girder Construction

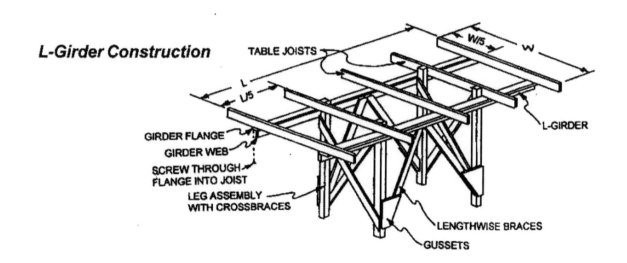

Chapter 4

ENTER TILTABLE BENCHWORK

What's a *TilTable? You ask.*

TILTABLE CONSTRUCTION

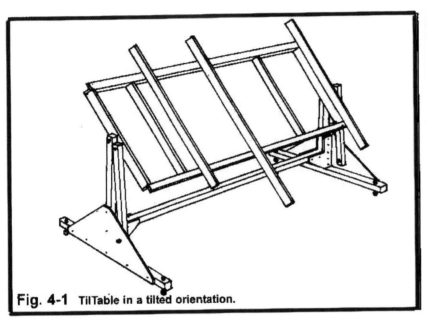

Fig. 4-1 TilTable in a tilted orientation.

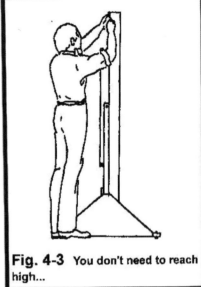

Fig. 4-3 You don't need to reach high...

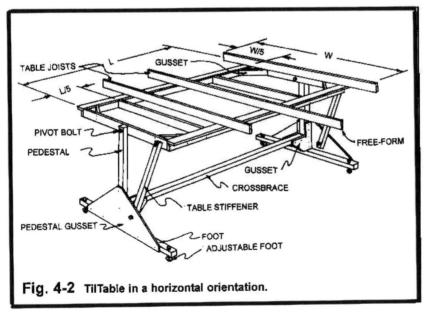

Fig. 4-2 TilTable in a horizontal orientation.

Fig. 4-4 Even the 'low' work is not *under* the table...

As the name implies, *TilTable* is a model railroad table that *TILTS!*

Now instead of crawling **under** the table to mount table joists, you remove a nut and bolt, and **tilt** the table *so the bottom tilts to you*.

Now instead of crawling **on** the table **or** s-t-r-e-t-c-h-i-n-g to reach the center, you remove **a nut and bolt,** *and the table top tilts to you*.

No mater what the job - fastening risers and sub-roadbed, cutting plywood on the table top, laying track, wiring, or adding scenery, you remove a nut and bolt, and the job is suddenly easier than ever before because you tilt the table, pull up a comfortable chair, *and bring the work area to you* instead of vice versa.

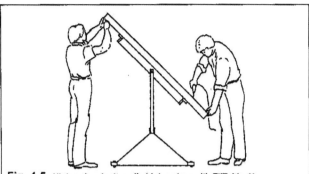

Fig. 4-5 High or low isn't really high or low with TilTable. You can always bring the work within reach - and sit in a comfortable chair if you desire.

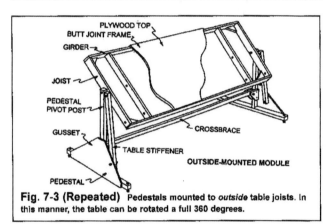

Fig. 7-3 (Repeated) Pedestals mounted to *outside* table joists. In this manner, the table can be rotated a full 360 degrees.

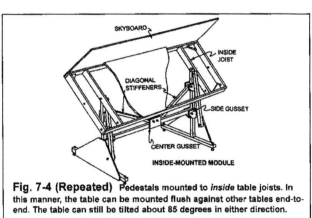

Fig. 7-4 (Repeated) Pedestals mounted to *inside* table joists. In this manner, the table can be mounted flush against other tables end-to-end. The table can still be tilted about 85 degrees in either direction.

With *TilTable there truly is no 'top' or 'bottom' anymore.*

The *TilTable* is so versatile that people who could never build model railroads before - the handicapped, the disabled, and modelers who couldn't crawl under and over the table - now have the opportunity to enjoy the FUN of model railroading like the rest of us.

Basically, a *TilTable* consists of a girder frame like L-girder benchwork except that joist-to-girder corner gussets are used. The girder cross-section is an 'L' or a 'T' so the table joists can be

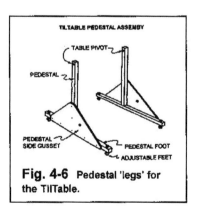

Fig. 4-6 Pedestal 'legs' for the TilTable.

fastened to the girder from the bottom through the girder flange - like L-girder benchwork. Using a girder frame retains the free-form arrangement of table joist edges - like L-girder benchwork. Of course, since you can turn the table *over* this is only important if you want to move a joist later. You can get to the screws from the bottom, but with the table *tilted, so you don't crawl under.*

The supporting legs' called '**pedestals' (See Fig. 4-6)** have built-in pivots at table height and can be mounted on *inside or outside* joists of the table, depending on what phase of building you're in.

Initially, you'll want to mount the pivots *outside* the table so that the table can be tilted full circle as shown in **Repeated Figs. 7-3 and 7-4)**

Later when you want to fix the table in position relative to *other* tables to complete your layout, *inside*-mounting may be desired so that all table ends butt flush with adjacent tables. Inside mounting still gives you tilt capability, but to a lesser degree. At that time you may add diagonal *cross-braces* along the length to increase table rigidity, similar to the lengthwise braces used in both butt-joint and L-girder benchwork.

This is not necessary while the major work on the table is in progress, but you'll want this extra rigidity once you place your table in its final location adjacent to other tables.

The entire table top, joists and all, can be positioned front-to-rear on the girder frame for better load distribution. Since tall scenery, and a good portion of the weight, is usually located toward the rear wall, you can *shift* the pivot support of the table slightly rearward to get better table balance.
(See Fig. 4-7)

At the same time this moves the *toes of the pedestal feet* away from the aisle. The best solution is to simply shift the pedestal rearward so that the pedestal foot has a 1 to 2-inch clearance to the rear wall.

To sum up, *TilTable* gives you these benchwork features:

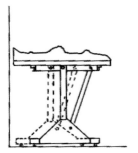

Fig. 4-7 Shift the pedestal for best load balance

• The table can be *tilted so you can* work facing the table.
• The table can be *removed* from the pedestal, if desired.
• Leg mounting is done for best load balance.
• The L-girder frame allows freeform arrangement of table joists.
• Assembly of benchwork is easier than other methods since you can *tilt* the work to add joists.
• The girder frame has the same load-bearing capability as L-girder construction.
• Since the table tilts, fastening, unfastening, and moving table joists is *easier* than other methods.
• All jobs of table population including laying sub-roadbed and track, wiring, and

adding scenery can be done by tilting the table and bringing the work area to you.

• You will never have to work *over* or *under* the table during the building stages of your model railroad.

• The table can be tilted vertically for storage with scenery facing a wall, if desired, for better protection.

Here are some other questions and answers on *TilTable* construction:

Will the table be strong enough if it can tilt?

(See Fig. 4-8)

Obviously, the table requires some type of support in conjunction with the pivots. That is the function of the table stiffeners. These are 2x2's which are pinned at both ends to the triangular side gusset of the pedestal and girder joist. Once these stiffeners are in place, the table is extremely rigid. The stiffeners are only needed in front for stiffness. The reason is that once a table is in place in a layout, the

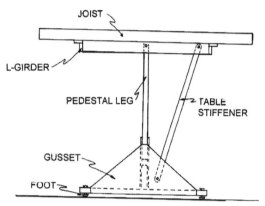

Fig. 4-8 Addition of the table stiffener produces a rigid table.

wall-side of the table is usually inaccessible, so unusual loads do not exist; however, some tables may have aisles on both sides, and then table stiffeners on both sides are a good idea. Some modelers may want to add them front and rear anyway. When the time comes to fix the table in the layout position permanently, this is no problem, for then the table may be tilted only occasionally. But in the initial stages of populating the railroad table, having rear table stiffeners will be unhandy, since each time you want to tilt the table, two sets of table stiffeners must be disconnected.

How WIDE can a TilTable be?

There's good news here, too, for you O- and S-gage railroaders especially!

With *TilTable* benchwork, table widths can be w-i-d-e-r than normal, but several factors must be considered in establishing the table width:

1. How low the pedestal cross-brace can be placed.

The purpose of the cross-brace is to provide axial rigidity to the pedestals. This is accomplished through the use of gussets fastened to the pedestal and the cross-brace. The gussets are normally applied in a triangular shape for strength, but never rise above the cross-brace.

This is so that an outside- mounted *TilTable* can be pivoted through a full 360-degrees; therefore, the longest table joist, as measured from the pivot center, must be able to clear the cross-brace.

By experiment, it has been determined that the top of the cross-brace should be no lower than about 10 inches from the base of the pedestal and foot unless metal brackets are used in the place of plywood gussets. This allows a plywood 10x10-inch triangular gusset to be used, but for slightly more pedestal rigidity, it is suggested that the gusset be extended up along the side of the post about 6 inches, but outside the swing of the table. I'll show you how later.
(See **Fig. 5-7 (Repeated)**

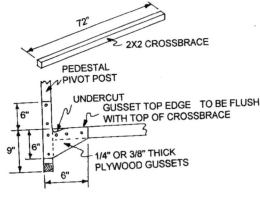

Fig 5-7 (Repeated)

So what does all this mean to table width?

With a 42-inch viewing height, 3- inch joist and a table pivot 1-inch below table joists, the pedestal is then 38-inches long. With the cross-brace 10 inches high, a swing radius of the table joists about the pivot will be **38-10-1 = 27-inches or a table width of 54".**

The subtracted 1-inch is for clearance to the cross-brace.
On the other hand, by defining the table width from the standpoint of **reach** above the table, for a 72-inch reach (assuming the longest table joist ends at that height when the table is tilted 90-degrees to an almost vertical position), the height from floor to pivot is 38 + 1-inch. This extra 1-inch is the adjustable bolt under the 2x2 foot = 39 inches. Then 72-39 = 33 inches, or a table width of 2 x 33 = **66 inches.** You will need to use metal T-brackets here in place of plywood gussets for the cross-brace.

As can be seen from the above considerations, the limiting factor in table width seems to be - *how low we can fasten the cross-brace.* Naturally, with strong metal L-gussets, the cross-brace can be lowered *all* the way to the *bottom* of the post and still retain post rigidity. Although this works, metal brackets *are* more expensive. You have to weigh the cost versus table width and decide. If your layout dictates a very wide table, then metal brackets may be the best answer.

2. Maximum table width due to your layout scheme.

If the width exceeds the width generated above, bear in mind that the widths discussed are for a full 360-degree rotation of the table top. If you can be satisfied with tilting the table only as far as the table cross-brace will allow (about 85 degrees), then TilTable may still be a viable technique for you. Certainly the comfort - or lack of discomfort - may be worth the loss of *some* rotation.

Pursuing this line of thought, if we *inside*-mount the pedestal, we know we have limited tilt to about 85-degrees, but now the height of the cross-brace is no longer a consideration in tilt except if the cross-brace contacts deep scenery, so a table could be about twice the length of the pedestal to the center or a table width= (38-1) x 2 = **74** inches. That 1-inch is for clearance to the floor. (That's a 74-inch wide module).

One further extension of the table width is possible. If you can accept less than 85-degrees rotation of your table, you can make the table wide enough to TOUCH the *floor* before it contacts the cross-brace. This tilt angle will be adequate to work on your table without ever crawling under or over it. With this approach, your table can have an outside radius of about 45 inches or a table width of 90 inches! This means that you could have a 90-inch wide table and *be able to reach any point on top or bottom* without stooping, reaching, or crawling - an exciting prospect for 'O' and 'S' scale modelers. **(See Fig. 4-9)**

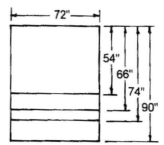

Fig. 4-9 Some table sizes possible with TilTable.

Table width has a number of ramifications. For instance:

a) *A large single table railroad layout.* **A 90**-inch wide x 72 inch long table is possible! That's 45 square feet, modelers!

b) *Use the other axis.* That is, you're not limited to tilting with the tilt axis parallel to the wall. Turn the table rectangular or free-form as well as some other things to consider:

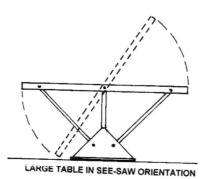

LARGE TABLE IN SEE-SAW ORIENTATION

Fig. 4-10 A seesaw orientation is possible, too. This works well with narrow aisles.

Turn the table so that it's like a seesaw. Then either the left or right ends can be raised. This works great with narrow aisles. **(See Fig. 4-10)**

c) *Single table* railroads, no matter how large, can be tilted when not in use and stored against a wall taking up only the width of the pedestal foot into the room.
How LONG can a table be?

With portability, a table should be no longer than 6 feet, but if you're not concerned with moving your railroad, then longer tables are possible using wider L-girders like 1x4 with table support mounting at the 1/5 and 4/5 points along the girders. This means inside-mounting of the pedestal on the *TilTable* flame. You will have the +/- 85-degree tilt capabilities and can still reach any part of your table from either side of the table quite easily.

But remember that getting a table through doorways, through hallways into doorways and down stairways, requires a table of limited dimensional length.

What happens after the table is 'fixed' in position?

As mentioned, once the *TilTable* has been populated with track, wiring, and scenery, you will want to fix it in position - perhaps relative to other tables - to complete your layout. At this point - or actually at the scenery stage - you will have to consider access to hard-to-get-at parts of your railroad - just as you would if you were building with any *other* type of construction. This is usually accomplished with strategically-placed **access hatches** which can be swinging doors or lift- outs. These can be regular wood frames built into the table with scenery on top, or the scenery itself can be cut with a saw after it is in place, and the piece lifted out when necessary.

Styrofoam sheet is a good candidate for lightweight lift-out hatches. An 18- to 20-inch square access hatch is adequate, and the opening can be square.

You have an alternative with *TilTable* that never existed before. You can build access hatches as usual - or - you can disconnect track and wiring connectors, tilt the table, and get to inaccessible areas, top or bottom easily.

For railroads that occupy the periphery of a room where there are one to four *corners, a fixed corner table* is recommended in which you can build access panels more easily. In this manner, all *TilTables* can be tilted easily without interference with each other.

For modular railroads, here are some other things to consider:

• More labor is involved in cable connectors and insert-able track sections. You'll have a connector set at each table interface like **NTrak**-modelers.

• Layout planning is a must so that turnouts don't end up at a table boundary or over girders and joists.

• Ingenuity is required to camouflage scenery breaks between tables.

Fun For The Handicapped?

Everything that's been said about *TilTable* construction applies to the guy or gal in a wheelchair who has full use of their hands and arms, or for those of us who don't bend too well. The railroad viewing height is exactly as discussed, a 42-45-inch height being just about perfect for someone sitting in a wheelchair.

With a little help from the local model railroad club or a woodworking friend, the initial ingredients of pedestal support and table top can be obtained. From there, you can follow in the footsteps of the thousands of other model railroaders and enter the fascinating world of design layout, track-laying, scenery, electrical wiring, locomotive and rolling-stock accumulation, and all the other interesting facets of model railroading. You may find you like to kit bash - build the myriad kits on the market today for buildings, rolling stock, bridges, vehicles, etc. - and add your own touches to your work as you go.

Or maybe railroad layout design is your favorite, and after reading the many books on model railroad layout, you create a railroad that incorporates your ideas.

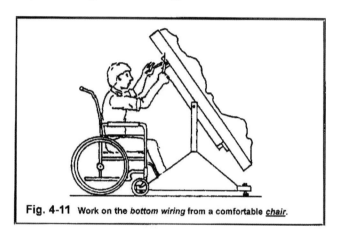

Fig. 4-11 Work on the *bottom wiring* from a comfortable <u>chair</u>.

Whatever phase of model railroading appeals to you, now you have the added capability of building your ideas into an operational module that you can enjoy - and with the knowledge that you can work ANYWHERE on your table, top or bottom, without undo effort.

Get Ready, Get Set - Tilt!

Now that you've been introduced to *TilTable*

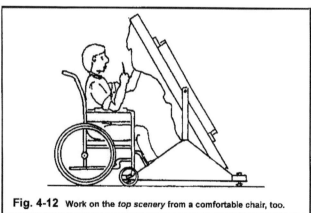

Fig. 4-12 Work on the *top scenery* from a comfortable chair, too.

benchwork, there's one more thing to be mentioned before going ahead.

Here's the situation - You have several *TilTables* adjacent to one another. You're about to pull one out one module to work on the scenery or wiring or track. You don't want to damage anything, right? So here's what you do...

First, I recommend that you put the following checklist on a card so it's available whenever you intend to tilt one of your railroad tables. Your model railroad is a complex piece of gear with wiring, track, and scenery. On that card

put the following steps:
(See the box-enclosed checklist).

With your checklist card at hand, you should have no problems when you want to work on your *TilTable*. In fact, now the job will be easier than ever before.

This sounds like more work than it is. This generally takes about two to five minutes, depending on how much free stock is on the table.

This, by the way, is the approach used by many **NTrak**-modelers, especially when they're new at the game.

CHECKLIST TO BE USED BEFORE TILTING TABLE

1. Disconnect all spanning sections of track between tables and remove them. It's a good idea to have these identified in some fashion so that a section can be replaced in the same location and also, the same end-for-end orientation. It's a good idea to have some standard location to store the tracks out of the way while tables are separated - in a box under the table, for instance.

2. Remove all locomotives and rolling stock. You may run them to another table, for instance.

3. Check for loose scenery - make sure it's fastened securely or removed, including buildings, people, autos, etc.

4. Check for loose access hatches - make sure they are fastened securely or removed.

5. Disconnect wiring cables at both ends of the table, and place ends in dummy receptacles or store cables out of the way. Be sure matching connectors are properly identified.

6. Move the table into an open position for work away from the wall - at least 10 to 12 inches.

7. Remove the nut and bolts at both stiffeners. Hold on to the table since the weight distribution front-to-rear may not be balanced.

S. Tilt the table to the selected angle for working comfort; use a clamp to hold the table at the angle desired. Two ways to do this are:

a) Add a clamping 'arc'. For Instance, you can have detent holes to insert the stiffener bolt.

b) Clamp between the post and girder joist. You can also clamp between the table stiffener and table joist. This method has been used successfully on fully-populated tables with no problem.

Sit Tight or Switch?

Up to now, we've described several benchwork construction methods: butt-joint,

L-girder, *TilTable*, cantilever, and shelf.

Suppose you've already built a butt-joint table or an L-girder table - but after reading this, you see some benefits to you in *TilTable* benchwork.

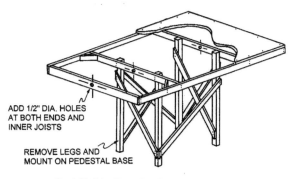

Fig. 4-13 Adapting a Butt-Joint table to TilTable.

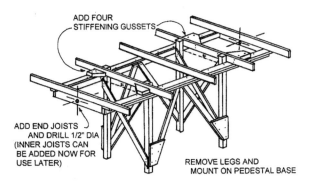

Fig. 4-14 Adapting an L-girder table to TilTable.

Can your existing benchwork be converted to *TilTable*? Easily?

Yes!

Existing train layouts can be adapted to TilTable with a few alterations. The decision to do this depends on the following:

1. How far along you are with your track, wiring, and scenery. If you have track and wiring in, and you're already into the scenery, a switch to *TilTable* may not be worth while unless you think you may have to move your railroad or do considerable remodeling later.

2. With *butt-joint construction,* where you already have a rectangular frame, or can subdivide your railroad to make several frames, the changes are straightforward. **(See Fig. 4-13)**

- With *L-girder construction* **(See Fig. 4-14)**, the changes are slightly more involved, but, for example, a 3x8-foot L-girder-constructed, fully functional railroad, with scenery, control panel, and complex wiring, was converted to *TilTable* construction in *one afternoon.* Now any area of the table can be worked on easier because the table can be tilted as desired, (See photo sequence at the end of this chapter).

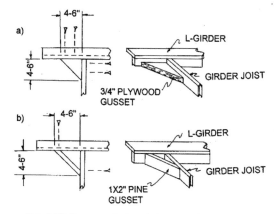

Fig. 4-15 Framework gussets to strengthen table frame.

First, you must add joists *between* your L-girders where you want the table to pivot, whether at the ends or inside or both. That's if you want to 'outside' mount initially and then go inside' when you 'fix' the table in place in your layout. Be sure these 'pivot' joists are fastened *solidly* to the girders. At this point, you have a rectangular L-girder frame, and you must add gussets in four joist-to-girder corners to *stiffen* the frame assembly **(See Fig. 4-15)**.

From here, it's like having butt-joint construction. Find the joist centers, drill 1/2-inch diameter holes, build a pedestal support structure and adjust the adjustable foot bolts on the pedestals to align the pivot holes in the pedestals to the pivot holes in the new girder-joists vertically, and insert pivot bolts. Install the cross-brace and cross-brace gussets on the pedestals. Then install the table stiffeners at each pedestal and unscrew and remove the old legs from the L-girders.

You must be willing to connect table-to-table with sectional track and cable connectors - like **NTrak**-modelers and model railroad clubs with movable layouts do.

If you have a single table railroad, there is no problem.

If your layout is just getting underway, or you have only sub-roadbed and track down, *TilTable* could still make the remainder of your building easier and more enjoyable. Remember, you still have a lot of over and under table work to be done. Why not do it the easy way -- with *TilTable*!

Here's how you can switch to TilTable:

Check out the 6-photo sequence at the end of this chapter for an actual conversion of a railroad to a *TilTable* in one afternoon – honest.

Find the centers of the joists you want to use as pivots, whether end joists or inner joists, and drill 1/2-inch diameter holes axially. Be sure that the pivot joists are glued and screwed solidly to the face girders.

Build a pedestal support as described in this book. You might even use the present legs and cross-braces in the new pedestal

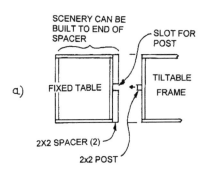

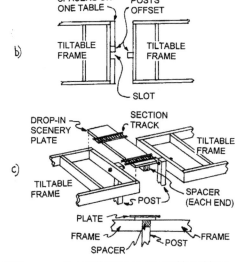

Fig. 4-16 Three ways to join TilTables to other tables without inside-mounting the pedestal posts.

structure. Mount the pedestals to your table ends.

Make two table stiffeners and go through the leveling procedure described later before drilling holes in the table joists for the stiffener mounting. Then unfasten the old legs.

You must set up your wiring with terminal strips or cable connectors at table ends if you have more than one table, and use insert-able track sections table-to-table (ala **NTRak**).

See the cookie-cutter sequence at the rear of chapter 5.

Now you have a TilTable, and your work will be easier from now on!

Butting Tables Together or Flush to Walls

It should be noted that all of the discussions have talked about outside and inside mounting of the pedestals.

Outside-mounting allows a full rotation of the table, whereas, inside- mounting limits rotation of the table to about +/- 85 degrees.

Some modelers will scratch their heads, jump right in, and try to figure out ways to use the table with *outside-* mounting completely.

Here are several ideas along that line.
(See Fig. 4-16)

a) Here the *TilTable* is to be flush against a fixed corner or end table. As shown, two 2x2's are fastened to the end of the fixed table forming a slot into which the post from the *TilTable* can nest. The spacers can be covered with scenery.

b) In this configuration, both tables are *TilTables*, but the same basic slot formation is used by fastening the spacers to the end of one table and leaving a slot opening for the post of the other table.

c) In this scheme, a drop-in plate is used between the two *TilTables*.

Scenery can be resident on this plate, and sectional track can be fastened to it for the transition from one table to the other.

One of the biggest advantages to the drop-in plate idea is that it allows the plate to be used as a spacer to adjust tables to available space in a room; along a wall near a corner, for instance. Thus, the drop-in plate can be any width you desire and help in adjusting your railroad space to the ultimate.

Maybe you can create other workable schemes for this flush mounting question. Good luck!

TILTABLE TILTED

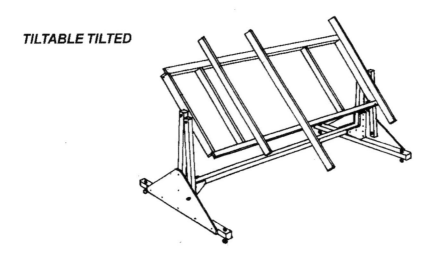

TILTABLE HORIZONTAL

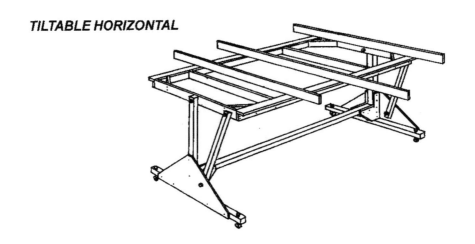

Chapter 5

LET'S <u>BUILD</u> A *TILTABLE*

To illustrate the procedure, we'll build a *TilTable* in N-scale that is a part of a six-table railroad **(Refer to Fig. 2-2 and the accompanying photo).** The scenery on table-A is rather desolate; semi-desert, but with a fast- moving river running lengthwise
through the layout, some reasonably tall hills (14 inches from the table pivot center), and one hill at the rear edge. We will make the seated viewing height about 44 inches. **Table A** in **Fig. 2-2** is the color-photo example of a *TilTable* module built by the author and used throughout the book.

Many of the **TilTable** dimensions work together or are functions of each other. You can establish the key table dimensions as follows:

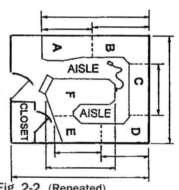

Fig. 2-2 (Repeated)

Fig. 2-2A Clay model (Repeated)

- Viewing height, **Hv**: 44 inches. **(See Fig. 5-1)** This can be changed later by altering the pedestal length and slightly altering the adjustable feet.

- **Pedestal length:**
  - $Hp = Hv - Hj - Hst - 1 - 1$
    where
    Hv = Viewing height = 44 in.

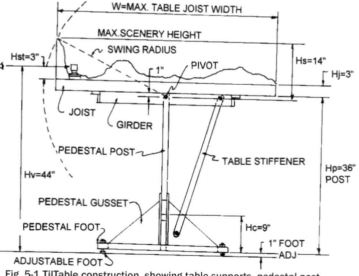

Fig. 5-1 TilTable construction, showing table supports, pedestal post, table stiffeners, and dimensions used in the construction example.

Hj = Table joist height (3-inch wide joists were used)
Hst = Rolling stock height above table joists (3 inch height was used in N-scale)
-1.0 inch for adjustable feet
-1.0 inch for pivot hole below the top of the girder joist.
In this example:
$Hp = 44 - 3 - 3 - 1 - 1 = 36$ in.
 (See Fig. 5-2)
Note that the top of the pedestal is flush with the top of the L-girder frame and the bottom is flush with the bottom of the pedestal gusset and foot).

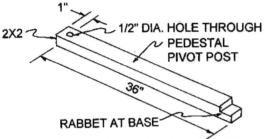

Fig. 5-2 Pedestal post showing the rabbet and pivot hole.

• **Table width**

On **Table A,** the longest table joist is almost 40 inches.

• **Maximum scenery height**

On **table A (of Fig. 2-2),** this occurs at the rear edge of the table and is about 14 inches above the table pivot.

• **Table length**

Table A is the longest table of six, and is 72 inches.

• **Width** of the pedestal foot

If we make the foot 4 inches shorter than the maximum table joist of 40 inches, the foot is 40-4 = 36 in. wide. **(See Fig. 5-3)**

• **Swing Radius (See Fig. 5-1)**

The swing radius is obtained by finding the diagonal of the triangle formed by half the table joist length

(W = 40 inches), and the maximum scenery height (Hs = 14 inches). Note that the maximum scenery height does not have to be at the table edge. It could occur anywhere, but it changes the triangle used to figure the Swing Radius.

Swing Radius = sqrt[(w/2)2 + (Hs)2] = sqrt[(20)^2 + (14)^2] = 24.5 inches approx. (where ^2 is number squared)

• **Cross-brace height, Hc**

Leave a 2-inch clearance to the swing radius.

Then the cross-brace height:

$Hc = 36 - 24.5 - 2 = 9.5$ inches.

Make it 9 inches for clearance.

Building the Pedestal (See *Fig. 5-3*)

Make two **(2)** pedestal assemblies.

Step 1. Cut two 2x2 pivot posts to length (36 inches).

Step 2. Rabbet the base to mate with the pedestal foot later. The rabbet must be along the pivot axis, and be 1/2 the depth of the post thickness.

Note; A 'rabbet' is an end cut or slice while a 'dado' is a groove.

Step 3. Drill a 1/2-inch diameter hole axially 1-inch from the top of the pivot post and centered on the post width.

Step 4. Cut two 2x2 pedestal feet to length (36 inches).

Step 5. Dado the center of the foot to fit the post width and rabbet. The dado must be 1/2 the depth of the pedestal foot thickness.

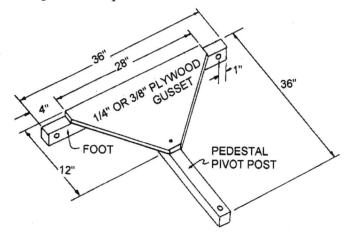

Fig. 5-3 Pedestal assembly.

Step 6. Drill a 3/8- or 1/2-inch diameter hole 1-1/2 inches from each end vertically through foot, depending on what diameter bolts you plan to use for adjustable feet.

Step 7. Cut two pedestal side gussets. The height should be about 1/3 the post height.

1/3 x 36 = 12 inches high and is not critical. The width of the gusset should leave about 4 inches on each end for the adjustable feet nuts and bolts, so the gusset is the foot width minus 8 inches = 36 – 8 = 28 inches.

Use 1/4 to 3/8 inch plywood.

Step 8. Join the post rabbet and foot dado. Glue this joint using white glue such as Elmer's Glue-All or Wood Glue. The foot must be 90-degrees to the post - otherwise the pedestal will sit at an angle.

Step 9. Clamp the post-and-foot assembly to the post gusset and drill one pilot hole for a #6x1-1/4' screw, 1-inch from the top of the gusset. Remove the gusset. Lay glue along the post and foot where the gusset will rest. The gusset base should be flush to the bottom of the foot.

Step 10. Replace the gusset, and screw a #6x1-l/4-inch drywall screw into the gusset hole and into the post.

Step 11. Align the gusset to the foot base, squaring the post and the foot to 90-

degrees, and clamp the gusset to the foot. Drill pilot screw holes at approximately 6-inch intervals along the post and foot through the gusset. Be sure to place one hole at each triangle peak and at the intersection of the post and foot.

Step 12. Insert T-nuts in holes in the *bottom* of the foot. These nuts can be tapped into the wood using a medium- sized hammer. Screw in carriage bolts to about a nominal position and add washers and nuts on top.

Step 13. Locate a position *on* the gusset 3 inches from the post and 3 inches from the foot. Drill a 1/2-inch diameter hole. **(See Fig .5-4)**

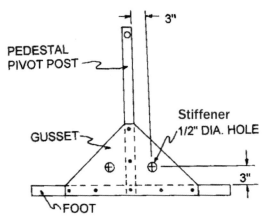

Fig. 5-4 Pedestal showing the position of stiffener pivot holes.

This is the pivot hole for the table stiffener. If you plan to put table stiffeners on both the front and rear of the table, repeat the hole in the gusset on the other side. If you want independently adjustable feet (and it's a good idea), two schemes are shown. Either one works fine. **(See Fig. 5-5)**

Or you can get suggestions from your local model railroad clubs who adjust feet all the time.
This completes the pedestal assembly. Make two.

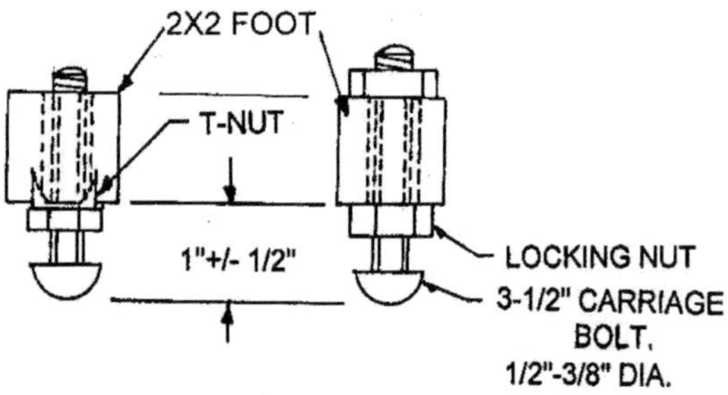

Building the TilTable L-Girder Frame (See Fig. 5-6)

Step 1. Cut two girder flanges and two webs to exactly table length. These can be either for a T- or L-girder.

Fig. 5-5 Two examples of adjustable feet for the TilTable pedestal.

Step 2. After sanding and eliminating all burrs, construct a 2-part girder outside of the girder by laying glue on top of the web (the narrow top edge) and clamping the flange to the web. Be sure the edge of the

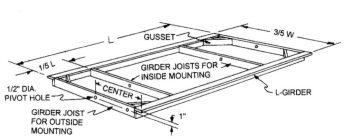

Fig. 5-6 A typical TilTable L-girder frame.

flange is flush with the web along the entire length.
(See Figure 3-2B - Repeated).

Step 3. Drill pilot holes through the flange into the web. Be sure the web and flange edges are flush before drilling. Immediately insert a drywall screw. Repeat at about 18-inch intervals.

Step 4. Cut the girder joists to length. Make four - two for the ends and two for later *inside* mounting.

Note that with *TilTable*, the girders can be mounted with the flanges pointing in or out. Since the table tilts, it is always easy to drill and screw into the flanges mounted either way. That is why a T-girder can also work well.

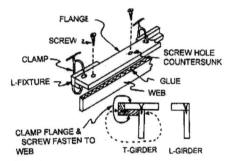

Fig. 3-2B A "T"-girder has about the same load-bearing strength as an L-girder -- with other advantages, too.

Step 5. Locate the center of the joists end to end and measure 1-inch from the top edge to locate the centers for the pivot holes. Drill a 1/2-inch diameter hole in each joist.

Step 6. Glue and screw the end joists in place **inside** the girders. All girder and joist edges should be flush at the ends.

Step 7. Measure I/5 the girder length from each end and mark both girders (to the nearest whole inch).

Step 8. Glue and screw the inner joists between the girders at the marked spots, inserting screws through the outside of the girder web.

Step 9. Cut four corner gussets from 1x2 stock. Make them about 6 inches long (this is not critical), and bevel the ends to 45 degrees to fit in the corners.

Step 10. Using a '**square**' in the corners, glue and screw the gusset in the outside corner. Repeat with each gusset. For best squaring results, square the frame, then clamp a spare 1x2 to a girder joist and girder. This will hold the frame square while adding the corner gussets.

This completes the *TilTable* L-girder frame.

Cross-bracing the Pedestal

Step I. Cut a 72-inch long 2x2 cross-brace. The brace is cut to table length.

Step 2. Cut four 1/4- or 3/8-inch plywood

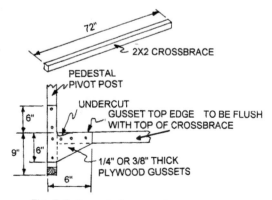

Fig. 5-7 Gussets for crossbrace.

cross-brace gussets to the shape shown. **(See Fig. 5-7)**

Notice that the 90-degree *inside corner* is undercut and rounded to minimize the corner stresses and provide clearance to the swing of the table.

Step 3. Assemble the gussets to the cross-brace (on one side only) with clamps. Make the gusset top edge flush with the cross-brace top as shown. Once the position is correct, drill pilot screw holes at thee points along the cross- brace through the gusset and insert screws. Do **not** use glue on these joints, as the cross-brace may be shortened later for *inside* mounting. By mounting the gussets to the cross-brace, assembly of the cross-brace to the pedestal pivot post will be easier.

Step 4. Determine the height of the cross-brace (allowing 1-2-inch clearance for the swing of the table, if possible. Determine the maximum height *of scenery* above the pivot at the front or rear table edges in order to determine the swing radius, R. For this example, the maximum scenery height is 14 inches, and R = 24.5 inches.

The cross-brace height is then, 36 - 24.5 – 2 = 9.5 inches.

Use 9 inches as stated previously.

Step 5. Stand one pedestal on its feet vertically and assemble the cross-brace to its *inside edge. Be sure that the pedestal is turned in the correct direction and that the triangular gusset on the post-foot assembly is mounted **outside**.* Once the post and cross-brace are at 90-degrees, clamp the gusset on the cross-brace to the post. Check the 90- degrees again, then drill pilot screw holes at 4-to 5-inch intervals along the post through the gusset, and insert screws.

Step 6. Repeat step 5 with the other pedestal.

Step 7. Add the two remaining gussets to the opposite side of the cross-brace with screws at each pedestal. Check the squareness between the foot and the cross-brace before drilling holes. Gussets on both sides of the cross-brace will prevent the pedestal from twisting. **(See Figs. 5-8)**

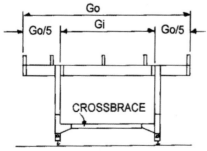

Fig. 5-8 Adding the crossbrace.

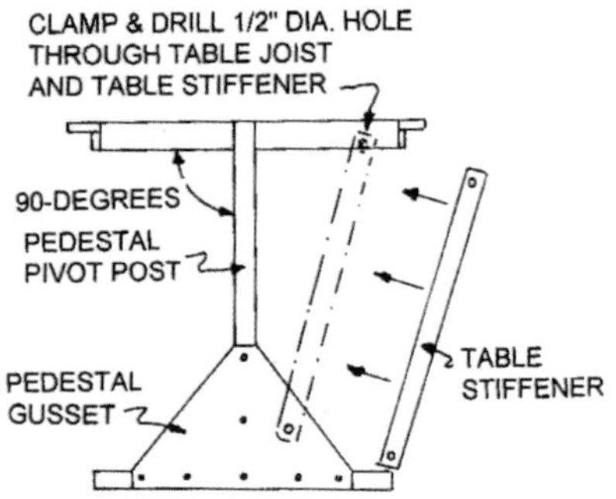

CLAMP & DRILL 1/2" DIA. HOLE THROUGH TABLE JOIST AND TABLE STIFFENER

90-DEGREES

PEDESTAL PIVOT POST

PEDESTAL GUSSET

TABLE STIFFENER

Fig. 5-9 Adding stiffeners to the pedestal and table joist.

Mounting the Frame

Step 1. Lift the girder frame into position between the pedestal posts and insert pivot bolts through the post into the girder joist at each end.

Step 2. Cut two 36-inch long 2x2 table stiffeners. This is an approximate length.

Step 3. Drill 1/2-inch diameter holes 1-inch from each end of the stiffener.

Step 4. Assemble the table stiffeners to the inside with 1/2-inch diameter bolts, washers, and nuts. **(See Fig. 5-9)**

Squaring and Leveling Your Girder Frame Table

Once before we discussed this topic, and the statement was made that leveling a table will be a waste of time UNLESS the table is in the exact location where it will be used.

So, if you're working in your garage, the floor is probably sloped rear-to- front for drainage. It would be a total waste of time to 'level' the table here since the final location for the table is somewhere else; therefore, I'll give you two methods of assembling the table to the pedestal:

One way uses the SQUARENESS of the parts; the other relies on the 'LEVEL' of the parts. You can use whichever method seems to fit your situation, although 'leveling' your table IS NOT valid unless the table is located EXACTLY where it will ultimately be used. If you were planning to take your railroad table to demonstrations in malls or at fairs, can you see what a waste of time it would be to 'level' the table at this stage? Enough said.

Squaring Your Girder Frame

Step 1. Begin by checking the squareness of the pivot posts to the pedestal feet on each pedestal. Next check the squareness of the pivot post to the cross-brace. These checks guarantee that you're starting with a square assembly.

Step 2. With the girder frame mounted on the pivot posts, tilt the frame until the table frame is horizontal or 90-degrees to the post, and clamp. Check both ends of the frame in this manner, and adjust by flexing the frame until this horizontal is obtained and clamp.

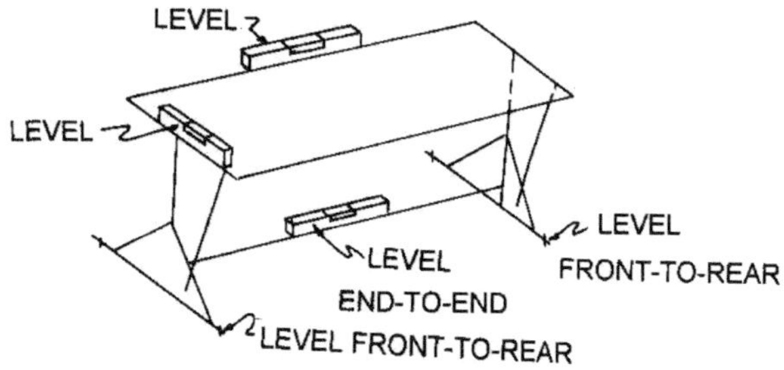

Fig. 5-10 Levelling the TilTable.

Step 3. Assemble the table stiffener to the INSIDE of the pedestal gusset with a 1/2-inch diameter bolt, washer, and nut.

Step 4. Pivot the stiffener up alongside the girder joist and clamp in place so that the 1/2-inch diameter hole in the stiffener is approximately centered on the girder joist vertical depth.

Step 5. Using the hole in the stiffener as a guide, drill a 1/2-inch diameter hole through the girder joist. It's a good idea to clamp a small piece of scrap wood to the outside of the joist over the hole location to prevent splintering when the drill breaks through.

Step 6. Insert a 1/2-inch diameter bolt, washer, and nut. Repeat steps 1-6 on all table stiffeners used.

Your table frame should now be square to the pedestal.

Leveling Your L-Girder Frame Table (See Fig. 5-10)

When you're ready to locate the table *permanently:*

Step 1. Be sure that adjustable feet are all in a LEVEL position, both front-to-rear and pedestal-to-pedestal.

Step 2. Place a level front-to-rear on a girder joist at one end.

Note: If you have previously *squared* your table, and drilled holes in the joists and stiffeners, two leveling methods may be considered:

1. Level the table using only the adjustable feet.

2. Cut about 1 to 1-1/2 inches off the top of the stiffener and proceed to add a new top hole in the stiffener as described previously.

Pivot the table stiffener into place against the side of the girder joist and tilt the table slowly until the bubble on the level centers. Try to center the drilled hole in the stiffener on the girder joist vertically and clamp. Recheck the level. Adjust the stiffener until the joist is level. Drill a 1/2 inch diameter hole in the joist using the hole in the stiffener as a drill guide. Here again, it's a good idea to back up the hole being drilled with a scrap of wood to prevent splintering of the table joist when the drill breaks through.

Step 3. Insert a 1/2-inch diameter bolt, washer, and nut.

Step 4. Repeat steps 2 and 3 at the other pedestal.

Warning: If you have leveled your table assembly and MOVE IT, the table may no longer be 'level'; however, you may be **able** to return it to level using the adjustable feet.

Table Joist Assembly

Step 1. If, from your layout, you know the location of the table joists, clamp one at a time in place, tilt the table upside down for easier working, drill pilot screw holes through the girder flange into the joist, and insert screws, one at each girder. Otherwise, place the table joists when ready.

This completes the assembly of the *TilTable* **for Phase 1.**

The table is now **outside mounted** so that the table can be rotated through 360-degrees for best orientation while working. Eventually the table will be fully-populated with track, wiring, and scenery. At that time, you may want to fix the table in its permanent location in the railroad. The pedestal may then be **inside mounted.**

Inside Mounting the Pedestal

At this stage of construction, you may have wiring and scenery already on your table framework. You may want the lengthwise ends of the table to fit flush against an end wall or against another table. It's at this point that you may decide to *inside* mount your pedestal, and here's how:

Step 1. Remove the girder frame from the pedestal supports. Set your table off to the side temporarily.

Step 2. Unfasten the cross-brace from the pedestal post from one end of the cross-brace *only*, and remove the gussets.

Step 3. Measure the distance between the outer edges of the inside girder joists, **Gi. (Refer to Fig. 5-8)**

Cut the cross-brace to this shortened length. This length should be about 2/3 the table length, **Go**. Or make a *new* shorter cross-brace if you think you'll mount the pedestals outside the table at a later date.

Step 4. Reassemble the gussets to the shorter cross-brace and post. Use the same method as before. Be sure to check the 90-degree angle between the post and the cross-brace, and the foot to the cross-brace before screwing the gussets to the post.

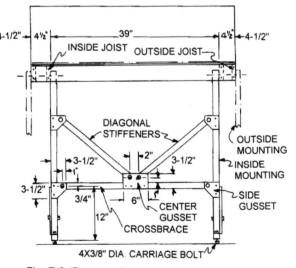

Fig. 7-6 (Repeated)

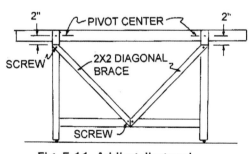

Fig. 5-11 Adding diagonal

Step 5. Lift the table into position between the pedestal pivots and insert bolts through the inside girder joists with the pedestals OUTSIDE these two inside girder joists. Add washers and nuts.

Step 6. Reattach the table stiffeners to the inner girder joists with clamps, drill 1/2-inch diameter holes in the joists using the stiffener holes as a drill guide. This is the 'squaring' or 'leveling' procedure as done previously on outside mounting'.
The finished table can now be permanently placed in the railroad layout.

The Diagonal Brace (see Fig. 5-11)

When the table is fixed permanently in the layout, you may want to add a _diagonal_ cross-brace to stiffen the table axially.

Step 1. Locate the center of the cross-brace. Measure a distance from this point of the cross-brace diagonally to a point 2 inches below the pivot of the post in each direction. Cut a 2x2 diagonal cross-brace to this dimension and cut the proper angled faces at each end.

Step 2. You can screw these diagonal braces to the sides of the cross-brace and post or to the face of each, but a better alternative is to make post side gussets of 1/4- or 3/8-inch plywood, and attach the diagonals to these gussets. That way, no through holes have to be made in the post. **(See Fig. 7-6 - Repeated).**

The *TilTable* benchwork is now complete.

Holding The Table In A Tilted Position

How do you hold the table in the angular position desired when you want to work on the table top or bottom?

Here are two techniques:

1. Clamp a large clamp (4-6 inch jaw) to the pedestal post with the 'C' section rotated up near the post.

(See Figure 5-12)
This works on either side of the pedestal post and depends on the weight distribution of the table.

For instance, in the illustration, the table is heavier on the right side of the post, so putting the C of the clamp on the right side allows the table joist to rest on the C of the clamp.

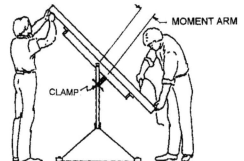

Fig. 5-12 Use a clamp to hold table in desired tilt position.

Notice, however, that the 'moment arm' in this case is short. That is, the weight of the table is bearing down on the clamp and putting high stress on the table joist.

This is the technique used on all of the author's table work when wiring or placing scenery. No problems have been encountered, and it's an easy technique to apply.

2. For those who like things more organized, this technique uses a plywood or plastic circular disk.

Measure the distance between the center of the pivot bolt and the center of the table stiffener bolt hole.

Make the tilt disk radius about 1-inch greater than this measurement. Cut a 2x2 x 4 inch block of wood and put a bolt hole through one 2-inch side. This block is used to space the disk to the table joist the same as the post.

Now when the table is tilted, the disk can be clamped solidly to the post. This technique has the advantage of a longer moment arm (the distance between the table pivot and the clamping point on the post). This puts less stress on the table joist, clamp, and post. **(See Figure 5-13A and 5-13-B)**

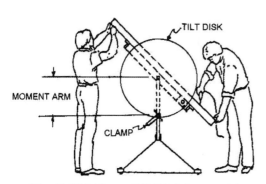

Fig. 5-13A Use a Tilt Disk to provide a larger moment arm and less stress on the table joist.

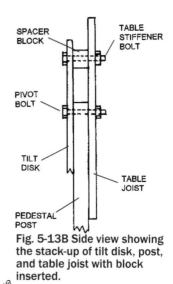

Fig. 5-13B Side view showing the stack-up of tilt disk, post, and table joist with block inserted.

The disk is only needed on one side. There may be a little springiness in your table frame with only one disk, but once clamped, you can always add just a clamp to the other post if you feel the need for more table frame rigidity.

The table will swing as far as the block in either direction, so almost 360-degrees of tilt is available.

Note: At the rear of the book is a material's list for a *TilTable* in lengths of 4, 6, and 8 feet, including all wood and hardware necessary to build a table.

Below is a sequence of photographs showing the making of a topographic top for a TilTable:

1. The frame is mounted and the plywood top is in place.

5. I'm beginning to add Styrofoam pieces onto the plywood to simulate hillsides, etc.

2. Now I'm starting to cut out the ribbon sub roadbed.

6. See, I'm already to the track-laying stage. (I just had to try this new trestle on the layout!)

3. Here I'm fastening a lowered section of plywood to the joists to form a riverbed. (Notice I'm not under the table...)

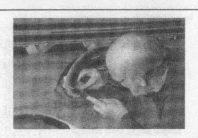

7. Track is now being fastened to the layout.

4. Here's the finished sub roadbed screwed into place with mini-girders (described in the text).

8. And here's an almost-finished TilTable complete with scenery, wild river, waterfall, three trestles, trees, and grass - *without crawling over or under the table to build it!*

One more time….

Below is a sequence of photographs showing the building of a TilTable module from frame-ready to Scenery added.

1. TilTable module ready for plywood top.

4. More track added to TilTable module.

2. Cookie-cutter or ribbon cutting for multi-level track.

5. Adding Styrofoam for Scenic hills and valleys.

3. Laying track on raised ribbons on TilTable top.

6. A scenery-finished TilTable module.

Views of Scenery-ed *TilTable* Module

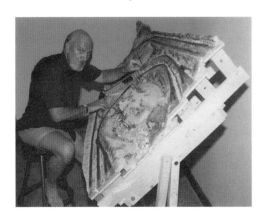

Chapter 6

LET'S BUILD A
CANTILEVERED *TILTABLE*

In Chapter 3, the cantilever assembly was discussed - as a table or a shelf fastened against the wall. This construction can be considered the most PERMANENT railroad structure of all, since it's 'built-in' and normally can't be moved easily - but we'll try to get around that point.

You can use any construction technique mentioned: butt-joint, T-girder, L-girder, or *TilTable*, so you can start with a known framework. Remember that butt-joint and *TilTable* frames have *corner gussets* which give rigidity to the structure, while with the L-girder frame, adding corner gussets is extremely difficult without adding the *girder joists,* so it's wise to select your framework carefully.

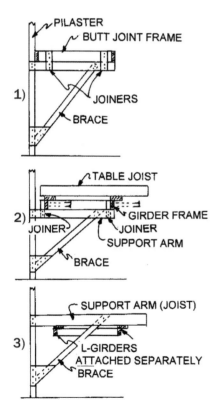

Fig. 6-1 General arrangement of elements for cantilevered tables.

Now, how do we support it and fasten the table to the wall, and - Great Classic Railroads! - what about *leveling* the table if it's built into the wall?

You see, it's what you do *after* the table framework that sets your railroad apart. For instance, you can plan and build a simple single shelf arrangement, or you can build a multiple shelf railroad.

You *can* build your shelf railroad without the use of pilasters'. Pilasters are the vertical 2x2's that fasten the cantilever assembly to the wall. Fastening the frame directly to the wall studs is a rather awkward proposition, since you'll have to support the table somehow while you fasten the table frame to the wall. There's a lot to be said for using a pilaster: it gives you a nailing surface on three sides, it can be used to support backdrop scenery for your railroad, and strategic location of wall anchors can give your cantilevered table great strength.

Let's discuss the 'standard' way to construct cantilevered benchwork and then look at the *TilTable* way since there are a lot of similarities. **(See Fig. 6-1)**

Assuming we have the table framework completed, let's look at several different arrangements of our elements. Here we try to break the basic cantilevered table down into the most logical arrangements possible.

These are:

1) a butt-joint table frame resting on a table support arm and a diagonal brace,
2) an L-girder table frame supported by the cantilever support arms by joiners with the table joists a third level above the girder table frame, and
3) a girder table frame attached *under* the table support arm. The table support arm in this case is one of the table joists, and is used as part of the cantilever assembly.

It should be pointed out that the second arrangement (the girder frame *over* the support arm with table joists above the girder) is highly wasteful of material. Do we really need *three* levels of support?

The third alternative seems to make more sense - using two of the table joists as part of the cantilever assembly. That way, we only have two levels of material, and most of the table joists can still be placed where strategically needed rather than put them all in alignment with wall studs; however, the second method is easier to build, since the girder frame can be pre-assembled, whereas in case 3, the individual girders must be slipped *under* the support arm and *between* the diagonal braces, so a girder framework can't be used without taking off the diagonal brace and supporting the table temporarily somehow. With those comments in mind, let's...

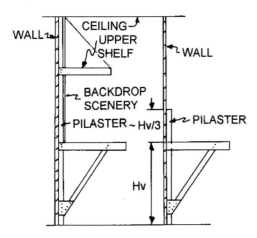

Fig. 6-3 The floor-to-ceiling pilaster.

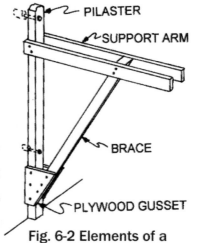

Fig. 6-2 Elements of a cantilevered table assembly.

Mount a Butt-Joint Table as a Cantilever
Build the Cantilever Assembly **(See Fig. 6-2)**
First, build the pilaster, diagonal brace, horizontal table support arm, and

support attachment gussets.

Step 1. Cut a 2x2 pilaster to the desired length. If your cantilevered railroad is to be a single shelf, you may not want the pilaster to be more than 1/3 higher than your viewing height from the floor. On the other hand, you may want the pilaster to be floor to ceiling for use as a support for your backdrop scene or a _second _shelf. **(See Fig. 6-3)**

 Step 2. Cut a 1x2 or 1x3 horizontal table support arm to the required length - this arm must be long enough to support the front girder of the butt-joint table. Cut two if desired - one for each side of the pilasters. This provides the cantilever assembly with more rigidity against twisting.

   It is recommended that the length of the support arm be no longer than the viewing height from the floor. Once the included angle between the diagonal brace and the pilaster exceeds 45- degrees, you may want to consider a four-legged table approach.

Step 3. Triangulate to determine the length of the diagonal brace - or lay the pilaster and table support arm at 90-degrees as they will be when fastened, and measure to the preferred attachment points at the base of the pilaster and the front of the support

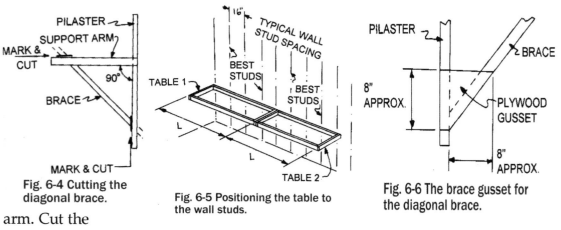

Fig. 6-4 Cutting the diagonal brace.

Fig. 6-5 Positioning the table to the wall studs.

Fig. 6-6 The brace gusset for the diagonal brace.

arm. Cut the diagonal brace to this length. (See **Fig. 6-4**)

Step 4. Establish which wall studs you will fasten to and mark lightly at several points throughout the height of the pilaster to be used. If possible you should locate these two wall studs at approximately 3/5 the length of the butt-joint table, and approximately centered on the table. **(See Fig. 6-5)**

Step 5. Design and cut the brace gussets from 1/4- or 3/8-inch plywood. (See **Fig. 6-6** for one possible gusset shape).

Step 6. Decide on the position of screws in the gussets so they will adequately fasten the diagonal brace to the pilaster.

Step 7. Clamp one gusset to the pilaster, drill pilot screw holes in the gusset and the pilaster, and insert screws. Repeat with the second gusset on the other side of the pilaster.

Step 8. Fasten the lx2 or 1x3 table support arm to the pilaster side. **(See Fig. 6-7)**

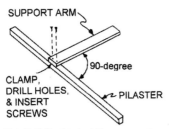

Fig. 6-7 Fastening the support arm to the pilaster side.

This can be done with the pilaster and support arm lying on the floor. You will probably have to clamp the arm to the pilaster while fastening. Be sure to check for a 90-degree angle between arm and pilaster before final pilot holes are drilled. If you decide on two support arms, repeat the above procedure on the other side of the pilaster.

Build as many cantilever assemblies as required (hopefully just two per table). This will be determined by the span of girders used in your table framework, and by the spacing of the wall studs themselves.

• Mounting the Cantilever Assembly to a Wall

Step 1. Drill 2 holes in the pilaster, top and bottom for lag bolts. Use three wall anchor positions if the pilaster is to be floor to ceiling. These bolts do not necessarily have to be the same diameter, but it's easier that way - a 5/8-inch diameter anchor bolt is adequate.

Step 2. Position the pilaster and arm

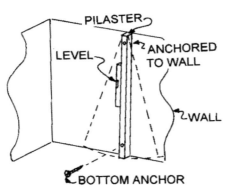

Fig. 6-8 Leveling the pilaster to the wall.

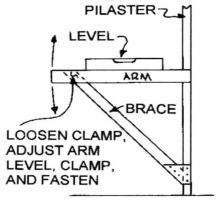

Fig. 6-9 Leveling the support arm.

assembly against the wall, that is, with the pilaster flush against the wall so that the bottom of the pilaster just brushes the floor. Locate the position of the top lag bolt, drill a hole in the wall stud, and fasten the pilaster to the wall, **(See Fig. 6-8)**

Step 3. With a level, check that the pilaster is vertical side-to-side, and *mark the position of the lower* lag bolt. Drill a hole in the wall stud, and fasten the bottom of the pilaster to the wall.

Repeat this procedure for all cantilever support assemblies needed to support one table.

Step 4. Insert the diagonal brace between the gussets and clamp the top of the brace to the support arm in the approximate position in which it will be fastened. Drill pilot holes in the gusset and brace and insert screws.

Step 5. Lay a level on the table support arm (aisle to wall direction), and check the level of this arm. **(See Fig. 6-9)**

Loosen the clamp on the brace and adjust the arm to level, then clamp the diagonal brace to the arm, drill holes in the arm and the brace, and insert screws. **Note: Be sure** to lay a girder lengthwise on top of two support arms and check that the girder is *level* between the arms before attaching the second support arm to the wall.

Attach the Butt-Joint Table

Step 1. Cut four (4) 1x2 joiners' to *join* the butt-joint table to *the* support arms. The length of these joiners should be the combined width of the butt-joint table joist and the support arm. Fasten the joiners to the support arm with two screws each with the joiner and the arm flush at the bottom. **(See Fig. 6-10)**

Step 2. Lay the table frame on the *support arm, and adjust* the table position end-to-end and front-to-rear. The arm must locate under the front face girder or the table will fall through without support.

Step 3. Fasten the butt-joint frame to the joiners with screws.

This completes a cantilever assembly using a butt-joint table frame.

Repeat this procedure for more than one table.

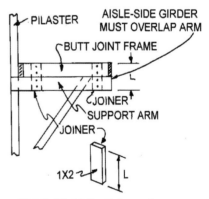

Fig. 6-10 Adding joiners for a butt-joint table.

Mount an L-Girder Table as a Cantilever

Building the cantilever assembly for L-girder construction is the same as for the butt-joint table above. The only *difference* is in how *the* girder table *is* fastened to the support arm.

• Attaching the L-Girder Frame <u>Over</u> the Cantilever Arm (Refer to Fig. 6-1, 2))

Step I. Cut four (4) 1x2 joiners' to join the girder frame to the support arm. The joiner length should be the combined width of the girder web and the support arm as above.

Step 2. Fasten the joiners to the support arms with the arm and the joiner flush at the bottom.

Step 3. Place the girder frame on the support arm and position the frame end-to-end and front-to-rear as desired.

Step 4. Fasten the frame to the support arm. Use two screws at each end of the joiner - two at the girder and two at the arm.

With the L-girder frame mounted *above* the cantilever support arm in this manner, the table joists can be arranged on top of the girder frame just as in the free-standing table case.

Attaching the L—Girder Frame Under the Cantilever Arm (See Fig. 6-1, 3)

This is a slightly more difficult arrangement to assemble. Since we want to mount the girder frame **UNDER** the cantilever arm, you can immediately see that the diagonal brace will prevent us from doing this. So, in this case you must start with the *individual* girders (we showed you how to build those in previous chapters). You can mount the cantilevered assemblies just as before. Remember that in this scheme, the cantilever support arm is actually one of the table joists in a girder framework, so choose the arm width used for your table joists.

Step 1. Locate the two girders under the support arm and clamp in place. You can place the girders front-to-rear at approximately 1/5 and 4/5 along the arm.

Step 2. Drill pilot holes up through the girder flanges and screw the flange directly to the support arm and table joist. No 'joiners' are needed in this case. Be sure the flanges of all girders face the aisle side so that screws can be fastened to the table joist easily from below. (With T-girders, it doesn't matter).

This completes the girder-under-the-cantilever assembly.

You can now proceed to place your table joists at any desired location as in the usual girder construction, except for the table joists used in the cantilever support arm positions.

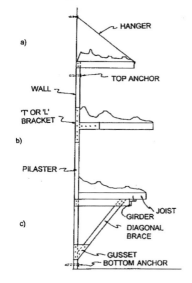

Fig. 3-6 Methods of supporting a cantilevered railroad shelf.

Build a Shelf Above (Refer to Fig. 3-6)

As mentioned, a shelf is simply a raised cantilever. The shelf can be supported from above using wire supports, below using the familiar diagonal support or even the metal bookcase brackets (if used with the metal pilaster sold for adjustable bookshelves),

It can also be supported with a metal T-bracket or L-bracket which spans a wooden pilaster above and below the shelf.

It is best to use the same pilaster for the shelf as for the lower cantilever assembly. By extending this pilaster, the entire railroad will be more rigid. **(See Fig. 6-11)**

Also, as mentioned, the face of the pilaster can be used to support a painted backdrop scene such as sky, mountains, and so forth.

The vertical spacing between the cantilevered table and the shelf must be chosen so that you will have adequate space for scenery, and you can reach between the two to work on wiring track-laying, and scenery, and there is space, if desired, for lighting under the shelf to illuminate the lower table.

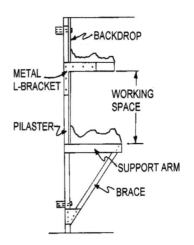

Fig. 6-11 Single pilaster for a table and a shelf.

TilTable Cantilever Bench work

You can use the *TilTable* for a cantilever and a shelf railroad. The same considerations apply as above for this technique.

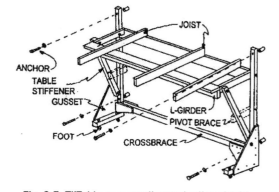

Fig. 3-5 TilTable as a cantilevered railroad table.

Build a Half Pedestal (See Fig. 3-5 - repeated)

Step 1. Cut a 2x2 pilaster to the desired length, whether the table height is for a cantilever or ceiling height for a multi-shelf railroad.

Step 2. Cut a 1x2 horizontal aim to the desired length (the table width).

Step 3. Cut two lower gussets of 1/4- or *3/8-inch* plywood, one for each side of the pilaster on which to mount the brace.

Step 4. Drill a 1/2-inch diameter pivot hole in line with the gussets on which the brace will pivot.

Step 5. Fasten the gussets to the pilaster with three to five screws each.

Step 6. Locate and mark the table pivot hole in the pilaster and drill a 1/2-inch diameter hole through.

An alternate method is to build two gussets for this pivot, an upper and a lower gusset, so that the arm pivots in *front* of the

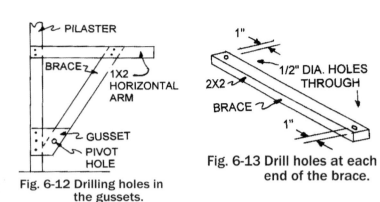

Fig. 6-12 Drilling holes in the gussets.

Fig. 6-13 Drill holes at each end of the brace.

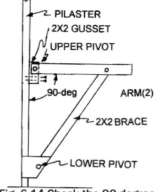

Fig. 6-14 Check the 90-degree angle between the arm and the pilaster.

pilaster. This approach makes the pilaster stronger since there will be no 1/2-inch diameter hole drilled *through* it, but only three screws holding each gusset to the pilaster. **(See Fig.6-12).**

Step 7. Mount the horizontal arm to the pilaster pivot with a 1/2-inch diameter bolt, washer, and nut.

Step 8. With the arm-to-pilaster at 90-degrees, measure and cut a 2x2 diagonal brace or table stiffener.

Step 9. Drill 1/2-inch diameter holes 1-inch from each end of the brace, and mount the lower end pivot in the gussets with a 1/2-inch diameter bolt, washer, and nut. **(See Fig. 6-13)**

Step 10. Check the 90-degree angle between the arm and the pilaster and clamp the brace to the horizontal arm. Then drill a 1/2-inch diameter hole through the am using the hole in the brace as a guide, Insert a 1/2-inch diameter bolt, washer, and nut. **(See Fig. 6-14)**

A third approach can be considered here, and that is to place the pivot at the CENTER of the table to be mounted. Shown are three alternative ways to provide a rigid center pivot arrangement: (See **Fig. 6-15**)

a) Screw an extra 'strap' between the pilaster and the brace so that the brace is held rigid. Drill a 1/2-inch diameter pivot hole in the brace 1-inch from the top. The table can be mounted with a pivot bolt, and fastened to a second hole in the strap with a quick disconnect or 1/2-inch diameter bolt, washer, and nut.

b) Cut a triangular brace gusset as shown and screw it to the side of the pilaster with four or five screws. Drill a 1/2-inch diameter pivot hole as above and mount the table with a 1/2-inch diameter pivot bolt. With this arrangement, a second bolt hole can be located along the brace gusset for a removable bolt which will hold the table rigid when inserted.

c) Use a long metal L-bracket with a 1/2-inch diameter pivot hole and disconnect hole along the horizontal leg, and screw the bracket to the side of

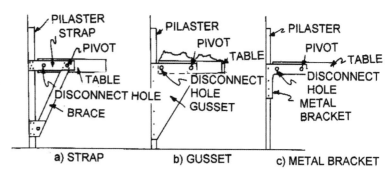

Fig. 6-15 Three assembly methods to place the pivlot center in the center of the table support arm.

the pilaster with about four or five screws.

Now why go to all the trouble to pivot the table in the CENTER rather than at the wall end?

A look at the illustration will show you the answer. **(See Fig. 6-16)**

With a *rear* pivot, the table pivots in a wide arc - the radius of the table's full width - either up 90-degrees or down 90-degrees, so the table ends up either high or low (not too significant), but you'll have to locate an upper shelf high enough so that no interference occurs between the shelf and cantilevered table when either is tilted; however, with a <u>center</u> pivot, you're back to a potential 360-degree rotation -- if you have outside-mounted the pivots and your scenery is not too high. If inside mounted, you still have about 90-degrees rotation, but always at viewing level.

Naturally the amount of tilt available for a cantilevered table or shelf is limited, but the tilt capability still makes wiring, track-laying, and scenery easier.

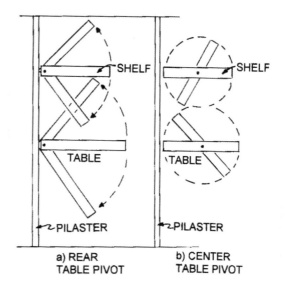

Fig. 6-16 Examples of pivoting tables at the rear and pivoting tables at the center for convenience.

The main limitation to tilt angle in the UP direction will be the height of scenery. Caution should be used in tilting the table or shelf up so that scenery *on top* is not crushed. Likewise, any construction *below* the table frame will limit downward tilt. This is the reason for the suggestion to center- pivot the table. **This completes the cantilevered *TilTable* assembly.**

At this point a butt-joint or L-girder frame can be made and attached to the horizontal arms at the pivot point in a manner as described above.

Build an Upper Shelf

An upper or lower shelf can be made along the same lines as described above. Just remember that if you're not interested in tilting the shelf, the three shelf support techniques described above will suffice. That is, supporting a shelf with wire from above, a brace from below, or a T- or L-bracket fastened to the pilaster. Also, the adjustable metal bookcase pilasters and metal shelf brackets can be used - with care, of course.

Chapter 7

LET'S BUILD AN
NTRAK *TILTABLE*

Loyal **NTrak**-modelers are shaking their heads. Why would you want to use *TilTable* construction in an *NTrak* module?
Let's see why...

Why the *TilTable* Works for NTrak

FIRST - ease of work.
TilTable makes it easier to work on the top or bottom of the module. That in itself is reason enough. But let's hear it from the NTrak-modelers themselves.

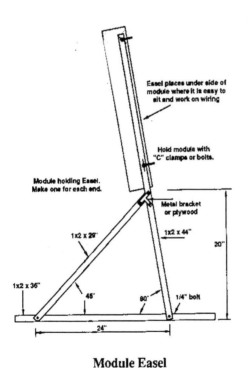

Module Easel

Joe Jeanes was installing several switch machines and associated wiring on his new yard module. Trying to balance it on chair wasn't satisfactory, so he built a quick pair of easel supports. Now the module is stable and the underside is at eye level while he is comfortably seated. This makes installation and soldering much easier. The framework is made of 1" x 2" lumber and the module can be either bolted to the frame or just held with "C" clamps.

(Reprinted with permission of NTrak Newsletter, 2424 Altaras Rd, Atascadero, CA 93422)

Fig. 7-1 A module 'easel' by NTrak-er, Joe Jeanes

Page 3 of '**The NTrak Module How To Book**" says, 'Another advantage (of the module) is that '*the module can be turned on its side or upside down, making working on it much easier, the light better, and with no hot solder dropping on the worker*'. The module can be brought to another part of the house where the rest of the family is, or taken outside when a smelly job needs doing". And look at the **May/June 1992 NTrak Newsletter, page 6. (See Fig. 7-1)**

Joe Jeanes built a special 'easel' to hold his module '*so that he could wire the bottom*'. Joe knew how important it is to get to the bottom of a module easily without crawling under. With the work and materials he put into his easel, he could have built a *TilTable* version of his **NTrak** module, and tilted the module any way he wanted. (Of course, *TilTable* construction was not available at that time).

Thanks, to Joe and the **NTrak** Newsletter.

I couldn't say it better myself!

Those **NTrak** examples show how important it is to be able to get to the bottom or top of the module *easily*. With *TilTable* construction, you simply pull the bolt from the table stiffeners and tilt the table to any position necessary to work on your module - *while seated in a comfortable chair*. When you're finished, the table can be leveled and the bolts reinserted.

And doing the work on a module in <u>any sequence</u> is a plus.

With regular NTrak modules, how do you work on the wiring once you have scenery on top?

Crawl under? Lay the module on its side? (Yes to both of the above). However, with *TilTable* construction, you can do the work in any sequence - and go *back* again if necessary by merely pulling a bolt free and tilting the table as desired.

SECOND - legs.

The "**NTrak** Module 'How to' Book", page 13, suggests that "Legs should be marked for the corner they belong to. Others may have to assemble your module at some time. Make it easy for them, and yourself."

With *TilTable*, the pedestals are <u>interchangeable</u> and require only that a pivot bolt and table stiffener bolt be inserted. Note that the module can be attached to the pedestal while at about 90-degrees (with module almost vertical), so it is easy to insert pivot bolts - without ducking under the module.

Other Considerations

Further along you'll see a scheme to quick-disconnect the pedestal assembly including cross-bracing. Also devised is a nesting arrangement of the pedestals and cross-brace under the module frame like many do in **NTrak** now. Leveling is straightforward with the four independently adjustable table feet at the

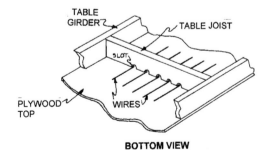

Fig. 7-2 Running wires under the NTrak module.

foot end of the pedestal frame like you do with **NTrak** legs now. The same clamping arrangements between modules now in use in **NTrak** can be applied to a *TilTable* module.

For wiring that runs along the bottom of the plywood sheet, the inside table joists can have clearance slots cut on the topside so that wires can run through joists without interference. **(See Fig. 7-2)**

Be sure these slots are *rounded at* the bottom to reduce stresses in the joist. Inside joists are used so that pivot bolts won't protrude outside the joists, and bolt holes don't have to be counter-sunk in an outside joist, weakening the hole and making it possible to break through the hole with hard handling.

On the other hand, inside joists are so close to the ends that it may be better to bring wires off the module at this inside joist. Then no slots are needed. **(See Figs. 7-3 and 7-4)**

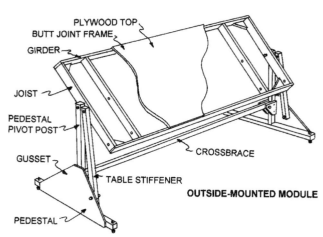

Fig. 7-3 An outside-mounted TilTable NTrak module. This is good mounting when you're working on wiring and scenery.

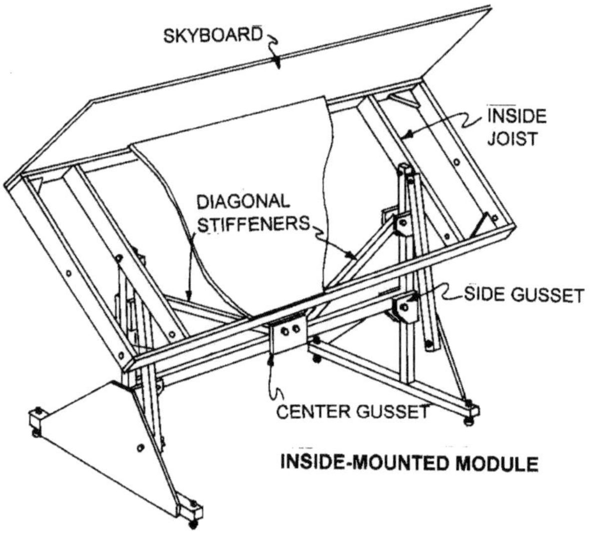

Fig. 7-4 An inside-mounted TilTable NTrak module. This mounting might be necessary if you're joining your module with others end-to-end.

Skyboards
(See *Figs- 7-4 and 7-5*)

The skyboard can be detached when moving the module. Since you can easily tilt the module while mounted on the pedestal, bolt and wing nut sets can be used through the rear girder to attach or detach the skyboard. Another scheme is a nesting technique like some **NTrak**-modelers use today. This scheme uses the skyboard as a structural part of the assembly. You'll see this later in the chapter.

Also, with proper sizing, the skyboard may be used to hold this nested pedestal and cross-brace assembly in place during moving, but this technique provides no protection for your scenery.

Scenery

Being able to tilt your module to get at scenery or wiring is a great advantage during the building phases of your module. It's nice to be able to tilt to any angle and spray paint scenery hills with the spray horizontal, and useful when 'weathering' the track on a module, too.

General Dimensions of A TilTable NTrak Module

Any of the basic benchwork construction techniques discussed in earlier chapters can be used on an **NTrak** module, but the butt- joint frame seems to make the most sense.

For tables 4-feet in length or longer, inside table joists give good top support, provide a pivot point for a *TilTable* arrangement of the module frame and minimize table sag tendencies.

Using *TilTable* construction on **NTrak** modules is done as follows:

Step 1. Build a butt-joint frame with table pivot points **(described in Chapter 5).**

Step 2. Build a pedestal with a cross-brace made for outside mounting **(described in Chapter 5).**

Step 3. Mount the module on the pedestal and lay track, wire the bottom, and add scenery to the top (all while *outside-mounted),* being able to tilt the table to any orientation desired.

Step 4. Once the main work is finished, remove the table, shorten the cross-brace for *inside-mounting,* and remount the table using the *inside* joists for pivot points for the module.

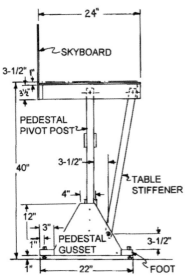

Fig. 7-5 Typical dimensions of a TilTable NTrak module.

Only one cut and drilling of a new mounting hole in the end of the cross-brace is required to change from *outside* to *inside* mounting, An alternative is to *retain both* the long and shorter cross-braces so that inside or outside mounting can be done at any time, making it easy to work on the table, and still making it easy to mount the table for **NTrak** layouts.

The table can now be used in **NTrak** layouts. With inside-mounting you still have about 85-degrees rotation in either direction available when desired.

Now that we've set the stage, let's build an **NTrak** module.

If certain parts are sized correctly to start, the pedestal parts can be nested inside the underside of the module like many **NTrak**-modelers do with the 4-leg approach now. Even better, if you have two equal length modules, we'll show you how to nest them together using skyboards and diagonal stiffeners to hold the modules rigidly.

So let's build a *TilTable* **NTrak** module. We'll illustrate with a 4-foot module since that's probably the smallest length on which you would want to use the TilTable approach. Refer to the illustrations for dimensions. **(See Figs. 7-5 and 7-6)**

Making the Pedestal

Step 1. First, determine the length of the pedestal pivot post. Assuming a 1 x4 is used for the frame (which will be a butt-joint frame, by the way), the actual width of the girders and joists is approximately 3-1/2 inches.

(A reminder: Girders are lengthwise parts, and joists are perpendicular to them).

The 40-inch height above the floor referred to in the **NTrak** literature refers to the track height, so we'll subtract 1/2 inch for track and roadbed. Then we'll subtract another 1/2 inch for the flat top thickness of the plywood (assuming you are using a plywood sheet on top). Now you're down to the girder and joist top at 39 inches, so 39- 3-1/2 = 35-1/2 inches, the distance from the floor to the bottom edge of the joist. Locate the center of a pivot hole 1-inch above this bottom edge centered on the joist length.

Now we can size the length of the pedestal pivot post.

Extend the top of the post 1-inch above the pivot hole. Also leave 1-inch from the bottom of the post to the floor for the adjustable foot.

The pivot post overall length then is 35-1/2 + 1 + 1 - 1 = 36-1/2 inches. Make two pivot posts of 2x2 stock.

Step 2. Cut two (2) 2x2 foot parts. Make the length so they will fit *inside* the module frame front to rear. About 22 inches is a good length and provides a slight clearance to the frame.

Step 3. To *nest* the two pedestal assemblies later for moving, the pedestals must be offset from the center of the foot so that they will clear any gussets mounted to the post sides and the posts themselves, Nesting will be described later.

Offset the pedestal on the foot by 1-inch. As explained in the *TilTable* section **(Chapter 5),** *dado* the foot and *rabbet* the post to fit together. You can glue and screw these parts together. Be sure the post is 90-degrees to the foot.

Note: Remember that a dado is a groove and a rabbet is an edge cut.

Step 4. Make pedestal gussets of 1/4 or 3/8 inch plywood. Make the gusset so that the base is 3 inches from the end of the foot on each end. That's 22 – 6 = 16-inch-wide gusset. The height of the gusset is 12 inches, an arbitrary height, but adequate for rigidity. If you make the peak 4 inches wide, you can make the diagonal cuts on the gusset identical.

Step 5. Glue and screw the gusset to the post assembly being sure the gusset is centered on the foot with 3-inch clearance at both ends. Be sure the post is 90-degrees to the foot when the gusset is attached.

Step 6. Locate a pivot center on the gusset for the table stiffener. Measure 3-1/2 inches from the foot and 3-1/2 inches from the post. Drill a 1/2-inch diameter hole in the gusset at this location. Back up the plywood with a wood scrap so it doesn't splinter when the drill breaks through. Table stiffeners are only needed on the aisle side unless your module is unusually heavy in the rear. The aisle side is where you're most exposed to someone putting heavy weight on the module. It's hard to bear down on the module in the rear with the skyboard in place.

Step 7. Locate centers for the adjustable feet bolts 1-inch from the ends of the foot and centered on the 2x2. Drill a hole the size of your adjustable bolt (a 4x3/8-inch diameter carriage bolt works well here). Insert a 'T-nut' in the bottom of the hole, insert a carriage bolt from the bottom, and add a wing nut on top.

Step 8. Make two table stiffeners to 32-inch length. Drill 1/2-inch diameter holes 1-inch from each end. Attach them to the gusset in the same plane as the pivot post. Use 2-1/2x1/2-inch diameter bolts and nuts. Wing nuts are not necessary here since the table stiffeners will not be removed from the gussets.

Make two pedestal assemblies.

Making the Pedestal Cross-brace and Diagonal Stiffeners (See *Fig. 7-6*)

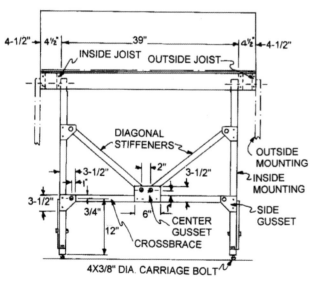

Fig. 7-6 The cross-brace and gusset arrangement.

Initially, the cross-brace is 48 inches long since it will span the table to fasten to *outside-mounted* pedestal posts. Here we will discuss the length when *inside* mounted.

Step 1. Since the 2x2 posts are actually about 1-1/2-inch square, the 2x2 horizontal cross-brace length will be the distance between the inside faces of the inside pivot joists minus 2x the thickness of the pivot posts or 39-1/2 - 1-1/2 = 36 inches. Cut the cross-brace to length and drill two 1/2-inch diameter holes 1-inch from each end.

Step 2. Make eight post side gussets with 1/2-inch diameter holes as shown.
 (See Fig. 7-7)

Step 3. Locate a side gusset so that the pivot hole is 12-inches from the base of the pivot post. Mount one gusset to each pivot post with two screws.

Step 4. Mount two gussets on the opposite side of the pivot posts with the cross-brace in place and a 2-1/2x1/2- inch diameter bolt through both gussets and the cross-brace. This will insure that the last gussets are located properly for insertion of bolts later when quick-disconnecting or setting up. Use wing nuts on these bolts for quick disconnect.

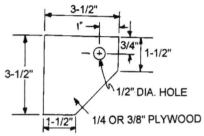

**Fig. 7-7 Post side gussets --
8 required.**

Step 5. Make two gussets for the center of the cross-brace as shown.
   (Refer to **Fig. 7-6)**

Mount one gusset to the cross-brace exactly in the center with the bottom of the gusset flush with the bottom of the cross-brace using four screws.

Step 6. Cut two 2x2 diagonal stiffeners 22-inches in length. Drill 1/2- inch diameter holes 1-inch from each end of both, then round the ends around the holes.

Step 7. Mount the diagonal stiffeners in the holes in the center cross-brace gusset with 2-l/2x1/2-inch diameter bolts and attach the opposite side gusset to the cross-brace with screws so that the diagonals are square. Use wing nuts on these bolts.

Step 8. With the post of each pedestal at 90-degrees to the cross-brace, clamp a scrap board across the post and the cross-brace to hold this 90-degrees, position the diagonal so that you can insert a 2-1/2x1/2-inch diameter bolt through a post side gusset and the diagonal, and attach the gusset to the post with screws.
   Repeat for both diagonals.

Step 9. With the bolt still through the gusset and the diagonal, locate the opposite gussets and attach with screws while the bolt is through both the gussets and the diagonal. Use wing nuts on these bolts.

The pedestal assembly is now complete and will stand alone.

Making the Module Frame (See *Fig. 7-8*)

Step 1. Make two 1x4, 1-depth *girders* to a length of 48 inches exactly.

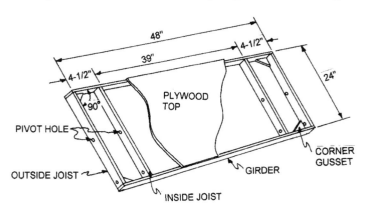

Fig. 7-8 The module frame for an NTrak TilTable.

Step 2. Make four *1x4 joists* to 24 - (2x thickness of 1x4) approximately 22-1/4-inches. **Step 3.** Drill a 1/2-inch diameter hole 1-inch from the bottom and centered on the length of all four joists. **Step 4.** Assemble the rectangular frame with outside joists and girders using glue and screws. Be sure the pivot holes are 1-inch from the bottom. Be sure the angle between the joist and the girder is 90-degrees.

Step 5. Since we want to *nest* the finished pedestal inside the module, the inside pivot joists on the module must be located in from each end so that the pedestal plus the adjustable foot will fit between them. This distance will be 36- 1/2 + 1 = 37-1/2 inches, but for ample clearance let's make it 39 inches. By the way, we want to use these inside joists so that pivot bolts don't stick out of the frame at each end - otherwise, we'd use the end joists as pivots.

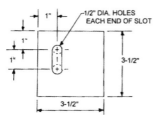

Fig. 7-9 Holding Blocks for restraining nested parts in the module.

Again, the inside edge of the inside joists will be 39 inches apart. Then this surface on each joist from the outside edge of the module is:

(48- 39)/2 = 4-1/2 inches. **(Refer to Fig. 7-6 or 7-8)**

Measure 4-1/2 inch from each end on both girders. Mount the inside joists with glue and two screws on each side. Be sure the pivot hole is 1-inch from the bottom edge.

Step 6. Add four corner gussets to the outside joists and girders. Refer to the corner gussets in **Chapter 6**. Be sure the girder-to-joist angle is 90-degrees. You can screw a 2x4-foot plywood sheet to the top unless you plan to use 'open grid' roadbed construction.

Step 7. In order to retain nested parts in place under the module, make two (2) 1x4 blocks 3-1/2x3-l/2 square. Drill 1/2-inch diameter holes and open into a slot in both parts. **(See Fig. 7-9)**

Step 8. Measure 2 feet from one end of each girder (from the *same* end of the module). Locate the blocks as shown with one slot *horizontal* nearest the top, and one with the slot *vertical* nearest to the girder. Glue both sides against the plywood base and the girder side, and screw two #8x1-l/2-inch screws into the blocks from outside the girders.

(See Fig. 7-11, 7-12, and 7-13 at the end of this chapter)
This completes the module frame.

Final Assembly of Pedestal and Module

With two equal length modules, you can nest them with scenery facing each other. Check to be certain no scenery from one module interferes with scenery from the other module. This may take some preplanning.

Step 1. With the pedestal assembly standing on the floor, lift the module frame in an almost vertical orientation (so the frame will clear the crossbrace) into position between the posts and insert 3x1/2-inch diameter pivot bolts through the posts toward the joists. When the bolt protrudes from the inside joist, add a wing nut or nut.

Step 2. Orient the module frame at 90-degrees to the pivot post and clamp. The module should be horizontal.

Step 3. Pivot the table stiffener against the table joist toward the front- side girder, and center the hole in the stiffener on the width of the joist. Clamp in place.

Step 4. Drill a 1/2-inch diameter hole through the joist using the stiffener hole as a guide.

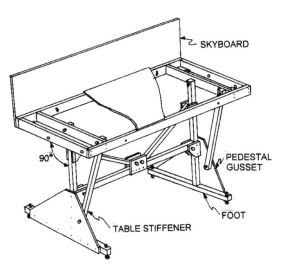

Fig. 7-10 Skyboard attached to the NTrak module.

Step 5. Insert a 3x1/2-inch diameter bolt and wing nut. Repeat steps 3 and 4 for the other pedestal. The module frame is now rigidly attached to the pedestals.

Making the Skyboard (Refer to Fig. 7-10)

Step 1. Using the dimensions generally used in **NTrak**, make a skyboard the height desired plus the width of a butt-joint girder.

Step 2. Clamp the skyboard to the rear girder with the skyboard flush to the girder at the base.

Step 3. Drill *two* 1/4-inch diameter holes 1-inch from the bottom of the girder and 12 inches from each end. Drill through the skyboard and the girder simultaneously. Insert 1 -1/2x1/4-inch diameter bolts and inside wing nuts. Note; A flathead bolt can be used with a countersink in the <u>skyboard</u> if no bolt heads must protrude.

.

Nesting Modules when two are the <u>same length</u>

Step 1. Remove both modules from their pedestals, and remove the skyboards.

Step 2. Invert one skyboard so the top edge is flush with the bottom of the front girder of the other module. Clamp in place and drill 1/4-inch diameter holes in the same locations as above (12 inches from the ends and 1-inch from the base). Repeat with the other skyboard on the other module.

Note: It may be best to drill the two holes in the skyboards with both skyboards clamped together. Then place either skyboard against a girder and drill holes in the girder using the skyboard holes as a template. That way the skyboards are interchangeable.

Step 3. Replace the skyboards on each module, invert one module over the other, and insert I - l/2x1 /4-inch diameter bolts and inside wing nuts.

(Refer to Figure 7-11)

Step 4. Attach one 22-inch diagonal stiffener in a table stiffener pivot hole in the outside joist. Due to varying skyboard heights, it will be necessary to make a new hole in one module joist for the other end of the diagonal stiffener. Locate the free end of the diagonal stiffener so that the 1/2-inch-diameter hole is approximately centered on the joist width. **(See Fig. 7-11)**

Step 5. Drill 1/2-inch diameter holes through the module end joist using the diagonal stiffener hole as a guide. Insert a 2-l/2xl/2-inch diameter bolt and inside wing nut. Repeat steps 4 and 5 with the diagonal at the other end.

You now have a rigid dual module assembly which can be moved by any method desired i.e., with rollers added or handles for two persons, etc. The stiffeners used at the ends can be used as handles.

Scenery is well protected by the module frames and the skyboards.

Note: Some **NTrak**-modelers prefer not to have holes in the skyboards where it shows. In

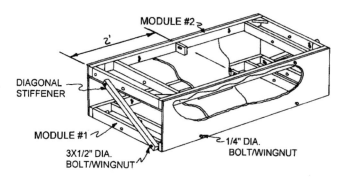

Fig. 7-11 Nesting two NTrak modules.

this case, you must devise a clamping method or a slot on the module to take the skyboard. Remember that if you used this bolt-on method, scenery on each module must be at least 3-1/2 inches below the top of the skyboard so that the board can overlap the girder on the other module when nesting.

If you have only one module, a second simple rectangular frame may be necessary (a 2x4-foot frame, etc.) in order to use this nesting technique. Otherwise, no protection can be provided for your scenery.

Preparing to Transport Your Modules (See *Fig.7-12*)

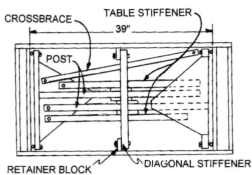

CROSSBRACE   TABLE STIFFENER
39"
POST
RETAINER BLOCK   DIAGONAL STIFFENER
Fig. 7-12 A nesting arrangement for two NTrak TilTable modules of equal length and width.

Let's assume your two modules are in a show and you're ready to pack up to go home. What's the procedure?

Be sure there is no loose scenery, rolling stock, etc. on the module at this time. This check is automatic with most **NTrak**-ers. *(But just in case it isn't, there's a ready-made check list in Chapter 4).*

Step 1. Remove the upper bolts from the front table stiffeners, allowing the module frame to tilt free.

Step 2. Remove the pivot bolts and set the module frame aside. It's easier to do this with a helper. If you have two modules, repeat steps 1 and 2. Be careful not to crimp dangling wires when you set modules on their bases.

Step 3. Remove the bolt and wing nut from the diagonal and crossbrace at one pedestal only. Lay the free pedestal down. Repeat at the other pedestal and lay this pedestal down also. Put the removed bolt and nut on the gusset.

Step 4. Remove the bolt and wing nut from the diagonals at the crossbrace. Set the diagonals aside for later use. Put the removed bolt and nut on the gusset.

 Step 5. Set one module on its base.

Step 6. Invert the other module over the first with the skyboards on opposite sides. Bolt and wing-nut the skyboards in place to the frame girders with 1-l/2x 1/4-inch diameter bolts and inside wing nuts.

Step 7. Insert the 3x1/2-inch diameter bolt and wing nut in the diagonal stiffener on the module end joist as shown. **(See Fig. 7-11).** Repeat at the other end.

Step 8. Nest both pedestals with table stiffeners attached and the cross-brace inside the inverted module frame on top.

Using one of the two remaining 22-inch diagonal stiffeners, insert a 1/2-inch diameter bolt through it and feed the bolt through the horizontal slot in the center retainer block. Install the wing nut loosely. Lower the diagonal across the nested parts to the retainer block on the other side. Insert a 1/2-inch diameter bolt and feed it through the stiffener and block slot. Install a wing nut, pressing down firmly on the diagonal to trap the nested parts. Tighten both wing nuts finger tight. A pad between the stiffener and nested parts will help keep them from moving around. **(See Fig. 7-13)**

Step 9. Turn the assembly over 180-degrees and repeat the nesting with the pedestals and the cross-brace. All loose bolt and nut combinations can be stored in the normal manner you would use with a regular **NTrak** module, or place them on gussets on the pedestals as the parts are removed.

Modules are now ready to be transported.

The foregoing ideas are shown to illustrate that techniques for nesting devised by **NTrak**-modelers can be applied readily to the *TilTable* module also. Certainly many will immediately see other and better ways to pack modules for transport or storage.

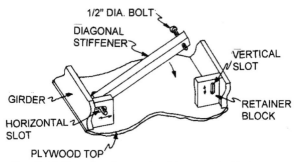

Fig. 7-13 Use of a diagonal stiffener to hold the components in place.

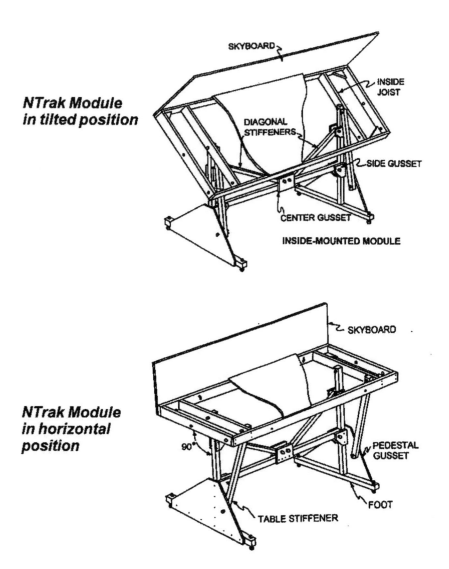

NTrak Module in tilted position

SKYBOARD

INSIDE JOIST

DIAGONAL STIFFENERS

SIDE GUSSET

CENTER GUSSET

INSIDE-MOUNTED MODULE

NTrak Module in horizontal position

SKYBOARD

90°

PEDESTAL GUSSET

FOOT

TABLE STIFFENER

Chapter 8

TRICKY BENCHWORK

Hello Down There...
That Low Scenery

For scenery that will be *extremely* **low,** special framing is probably necessary. For instance, a deep ravine **(See Fig. 8-1 and 8-2)** can be framed as a 'shelf' with supports to the girder frame at the ends of the scene. This may mean

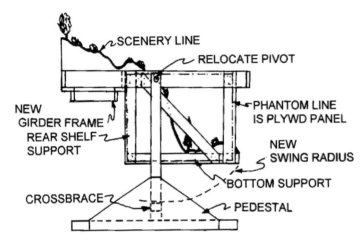

Fig. 8-1 A shelf on a TilTable module for extra low scenery.

relocating your aisle-side girder toward the rear of the table. Then you can build the shelf.

Of course, tilt will be affected. You may want to relocate the table pivot to the table joists as shown. With outside mounting, check the *swing radius* to see if you clear the cross-brace.

With inside mounting, you might also lose a good deal of tilt, as much as 45-

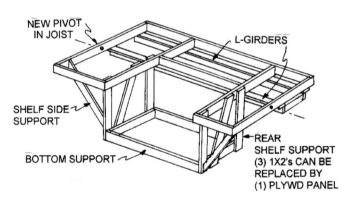

Fig. 8-2 Perspective of the shelf construction of Fig. 8-1

degrees. In either case, this will still give you the opportunity to work more comfortably, and you won't have to crawl over and under the table. This could be a good place to consider the use of butt-joint construction, as L-girder construction does not give much in the way of convenience here.

You might want to consider thin plywood panels as the sides of your shelf as shown **(See Fig. 8-1)** instead of the 1x2's **(shown in Fig. 8-2).** They stiffen the shelf well, and are easy to make. Of course, plywood can be *heavier,* so this may be a factor in your decision. (1/8- or 1/4-inch plywood is adequate here). And don't forget to use shelf side supports in front as shown to stiffen your assembly.

Another example of **deep** scenery could be a cliff or steep hillside built right *to the floor.* **(See Fig. 8-3)** The best way to handle this is to make this hillside framework *separate* from your table. That way, the table can still be tilted to work while the two frames can be butted together. If your *TilTable* has adjustable feet, you may want to add adjustable feet to your detachable scenery framework, too. That way you can always align the two pieces vertically.

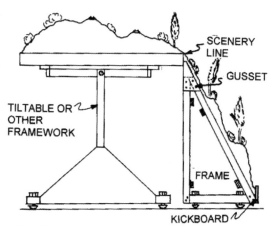
Fig. 8-3 Provide a separate frame for floor-level scenery.

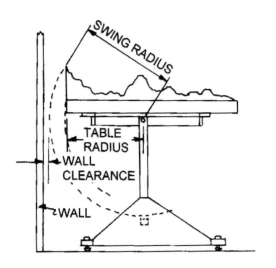
Fig. 8-4 Scenery height above the table is important in computing the swing radius

Say, you can even build your scenery framework to be used on either side of your main table.

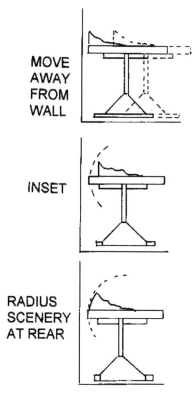
Fig. 8-5 Methods of protecting scenery when tilting module.

Mountains Out of Molehills -- That *High* Scenery

Most big layouts and many small ones have some mighty tall hills and mountains somewhere - usually tallest toward or at the *rear edge* of the layout. And herein lies a problem and a challenge for a *TilTable* user.

Scenery can be any height, but it's the height above the table joist swing radius that is of special significance when tilting the table. As seen in the sketch, if scenery extends vertically at the rear of the table to a height of, say, 10 inches, this creates a new larger 'swing radius', R, which must have clearance to a wall and also to the crossbrace under the table, for the table to swing past and down. **(See Fig. 8-4)**

Walls are the biggest concern, since it is usually in the rear of a table near a wall that the tallest scenery is built. Naturally, high scenery can also be built in front, so it must be considered in all clearances.

Wall clearance must be provided if you want to tilt the table that's against a **wall**. Some of the solutions for wall clearance are as follows: **(See Fig. 8-5):**

1. The best solution is to do all of your building while tilted out in the room - **away from walls.** If this solution is used, there is no wall clearance problem, since you will not attempt to tilt the table while against a wall.

2. Scenery can be inset from the rear edge of the table to create the necessary wall clearance.

3. Scenery can have a radius at the rear edge to create wall clearance.

4. The table can be built away from the wall by the distance necessary for clearance to this 'swing radius'; however, this is a wasteful solution, since it takes table space from your layout, and maybe aisle space.

All Together Now -- Joining Your Modules

The alignment of track and scenery between adjacent tables is probably of most concern to anyone building individual tables for the first time. **(See Fig. 8-6)**

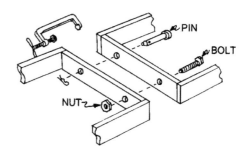

Fig. 8-6 Two methods of joining modules.

NTrak has developed a number of workable schemes to assure proper alignment, but generally, in a home layout, use a simple metal dowel pin or threaded bolt at two points on one table, and drill mating holes in the other table once both table edges are in exact alignment. Be sure to taper the tip of the pin insert so it enters easily. With the pin approach, a clamp is probably needed to keep the tables together; whereas with the bolt approach, you simply screw on nuts to take up the slack.

Take your pick.

The Sky is Not the Limit Anymore

With 'fixed' railroad benchwork, installing *backdrop scenes* like sky or rolling hills or far-off mountains is difficult. Simply *getting* to the wall behind fixed benchwork is usually tough, and usually requires that such backdrops be added **before** the benchwork goes in, thus limiting the artistic possibilities. Not so with the **modular** approach.

Modular tables can be moved away from the wall, and your magnificent scenes can be hung almost like paintings, or painted right on the wall or on mounted paper or poster board as desired.

Series or Parallel

Model railroaders all like to work at their hobby differently. You may want to work in Parallel - where you do all one type of job on all tables like laying track, for instance, before going on to the next phase, such as wiring.

The alternative to this is Series where you build one table, put it in the middle of your railroad room, populate it with track, wire, and scenery, put it into final position along the wall, and proceed to repeat the process, ie., build another table, etc. - until all tables for your railroad are built. In this scheme, you align the tables to each other as they're completed or nearly completed.

The series approach has a lot going for it because the modeler proceeds to DO every phase of model building on each table - track laying, wiring, and scenery. He completes all phases, becomes more adept at each, and in the process, his railroad gets better as he proceeds to build each module.

You can make your scenes look more realistic in room corners by providing curvature. In that manner, the scene appears much more continuous and realistic. And as we discussed earlier, with cantilever-type railroads, the pilasters make good fastening surfaces for scenery backdrops.

One More Combination

As a parting comment on the use of the *TilTable*, here's another suggestion that may be viable for modelers, especially those who are in **NTrak**. Some modelers may believe that *TilTable* isn't stable enough for them.
This hasn't been the author's experience. Of course, there's only one way to find out, and that's to build one.
But for those who don't want to use the pedestal in their layout, simply use it to wire and add scenery to your railroad table, and then mount the table on the standard

four legs! That way you get the best of *TilTable*, and a platform firmness with which you're comfortable; however, consider this: a triangle is the most stable building element there is, so the pedestal-and diagonal support create a strong table top support. A four-legged approach cannot do better than a triangle for a structurally-firm table.

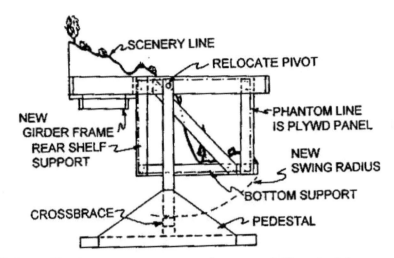

Extending your scenery beyond the table for a long hillside, for instance.

Chapter 9

IF IT *TILTS*, WHY NOT...?

Stretching the *TilTable* Concept

In the preceding chapters, we told you about *TilTable* construction and praised its merits. We'll call that phase *'TilTable* **Concept #1'**.
Now let's pursue the concept a bit further and see how it can be
s-t-r-e—t—c-h—e-d...

There's this friend of mine - we'll call him 'Big John' - an avid hobbyist and model railroader. When it comes to building engines or kit-bashing, or clever scenery, he s an absolute whiz! And BJ wants to build a BIG railroad, too. The trouble is, he lives in a three- room apartment with his wife and 3- year-old son. BJ has no space for his dream railroad...

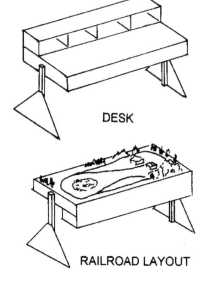

DESK

RAILROAD LAYOUT

BJ built *a TilTable* railroad.
But, you say, that takes space, and Big John doesn't have any space.
Ahhh...

Enter TilTable Concept Number 2
You see, BJ also needed a desk - or a Ping-Pong table - or a drawing
table - or - you get the idea.
What do you think BJ, did? You've probably already figured it out.
See Fig. 9-1)

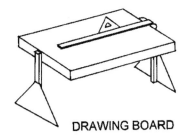

DRAWING BOARD

Fig. 9-1 TilTable Concept #2
Two-sided tables.

On one side of his girder frame, he built his
railroad - and on the other side, he built his *drawing table* - or whatever. He made the table top removable (or hinged) so that he has access to his railroad wiring,

when necessary.

But...now it's two years later and BJ has been dreaming BIG railroad dreams again...

You see, Big John and his family moved to a larger home. His wife agreed to give BJ a 12-foot wall in their new game room for his railroad. Now that's twice as big as his railroad/desk, but not nearly big enough to contain the 30-foot railroad he was hoping to build... (BJ DOES think BIG!)

This time, Big John's railroad takes a totally different turn (so to speak)...

Dial a What?
Enter *TilTable* Concept Number 3... Dial-a-Pike! (See Fig. 9-2)

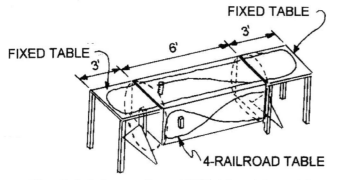

DUAL PIKE

TRIPLE PIKE

QUADRA-PIKE
Fig. 9-3 Multiple-railroad
end configurations.

Fig. 9-2 A four-railroad TilTable with end loops.

BJ built two fixed 3x3-foot reversing loop tables (in N-scale, of course) - one at each end of a 6-foot table. **But what a 6-foot table!**

Mounted on one pedestal are four 6-foot railroads, one every 90-degrees, each with a totally *different* scenery motif and *different* track arrangements - except at the table-to-table interface where tracks on each of these four modules are identical like **NTrak**. Each time he rotates the table 90-degrees, a new railroad module is aligned with the end loop tables. **NTrak**-modelers and apartment dwellers ought to love this idea! **NTrak** techniques are still in force here:

• Sectional track is used between tables.

• Wiring ends in cable connectors at each end of the table.

• Adjustable feet are used on each pedestal for alignment.

As you can see, John was able to achieve his 30-foot railroad in a 12-foot length of wall space: four 6-foot modules plus two 3-foot end loop tables equals 30 feet. So when John tires of the scenery and track layout on one module, he merely rotates his table to another of his four.

And look at this concept again from an **NTrak** standpoint. By building four separate modules, the modelers (and/or clubs) can mix and match their modules - and display a new railroad theme or layout motif every day of a show.

You can do it, too!

You can build *TilTables* with *two* railroads, *three* railroads, *four* railroads…
(See Fig. 9-3)

For example: Set a viewing height of 44 inches.
(See Fig. 9-4)

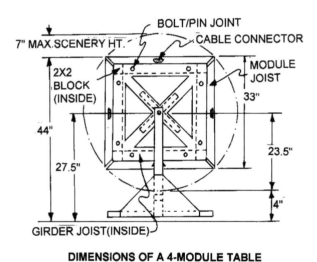

DIMENSIONS OF A 4-MODULE TABLE
WITH 44" VIEWING HEIGHT

Fig. 9-4 Details of a Concept #3 4-module table.

Since a multiple railroad scheme requires *outside* mounting (we want to rotate the table 360-degrees), the main restriction is on the height of a cross-brace to stabilize the pedestals.

Let's use metal L-brackets on both sides of the cross-brace for good rigidity to fasten the post to the cross-brace, and let the top of the cross-brace be 4 inches above the floor. Now we can calculate the maximum table width for that viewing height.
(Refer to Concept# 3 Table)

Concept #3 Table			
	Triple	Quad	Quad
View Height	44	44	47.5
Crossbrace Height	4	4	4
Pivot Height	30.5	27.5	29.5
Swing Radius	26.5	23.5	25.5
Table Width	46	33	36
Max. Scenery Height	3.5	7	7.5

Note that as the number of railroads *increases,* the *width* of railroad table modules *decreases* - or the viewing height must go up.

Included are the dimensions for a *36-inch wide* table in 'Quad' also - note the change in *viewing height* required.

See how a *three* railroad table compares to a *four-* railroad table. Numbers in the Concept #3 Table are rounded to the nearest half-inch.

A 36-inch table width in N- or HO- scale, of course, is big enough to have track reversing loops.

This means that you *could* build *four <u>complete</u> railroad modules on one pedestal* with N- or HO-scale *without* any separate end tables. This could be more exciting news for **NTrak** fans, who could build four modules on one stand for display and still have the standard through-tracks for Main line, Secondary line, and a track to join the separate layout on your module. That's four 6-foot railroads in a 6-foot space.

Let's see. If Big John has twelve feet to work with, that's...

But retaining the end loop tables also extends this scheme to the *0-scale-er* since he can build *wider* tables for loops at the ends!

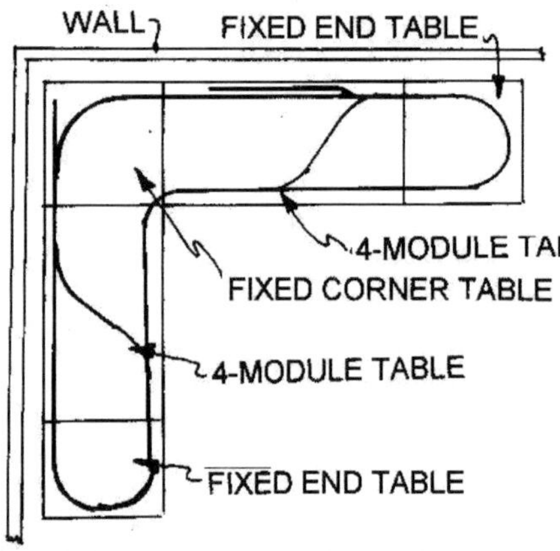

Fig. 9-5 A corner railroad with two 4-module tables, two fixed tables, and a fixed corner table.

Observe that *'without high scenery'*. You can build scenery to a height of 3.5 inches for the three- table approach, 7-inches for the four- table approach, and 7.5 inches for the 36-inch four-table approach.

Of course, if you want to add higher scenery, you'll have to reduce the width of the pike modules, provide more crossbrace clearance, or increase the viewing height.

There are *other* possibilities, too. How about a *corner* scheme? **(See Fig. 9-5).**

You can have two fixed end-loop tables, one intermediate fixed table in that corner, and two (2) (count 'em) four-railroad tables in between.

Now this may tax the imagination somewhat, but this means you have *sixteen* combinations of railroad scenery and track arrangements to run your trains through! And, *yes, admittedly* there is some set up involved to make this happen, but think of the operating possibilities!

A new railroad every week!

So - now that you're opening your tool *kit* and getting ready to **build** one of these Dial-a-Pike schemes, here's the *rest* of the story. You know how it goes. There's some good news and some bad news.

Well, we've told you the good news, and here's the rest...
As far as track-laying and scenery, you can still work on each **module right on the pedestal,** just like a regular *TilTable - but -* when it comes to *wiring,* you must *remove* at least **one** module to work on the wiring on any of the other three right on the pedestal. Or an alternate is to remove **each** module to a work bench or work area where you can set the module on its side and work on the **bottom.** Or another possibility is to hinge each railroad scheme so that the whole panel can be swung out to work on the wiring.

See? The bad news wasn't so bad, after all.

Dial-A-Pike Mounting Scheme (See Fig. 9-6)
Here's one Dial-a-Pike mounting scheme. Each *plywood* end plate has 'blocks' at the corners (on a four-pike scheme) on which the *table* end-joists of each module rest.

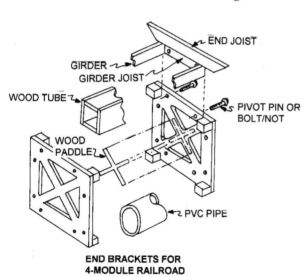

END BRACKETS FOR
4-MODULE RAILROAD

Fig. 9-6 Possible mounting schemes for Dial-A-Pike tables.

The **L-girder or T-girder** joists (yes, there can still be L-girders) under the table joists fasten to the end plate at two points by means of pivot pins held in place with quick-disconnect pins or with bolt-and-nut sets. Two retaining bolts are used at each end of the module, one at each end of the outer girder joist.

Several schemes have been considered for fastening the end plates together:

• A wooden 'paddle' can be made by slotting two 1x4 or Ix6's, joining them, and fastening the paddle to both end plates.
• A table-length PVC pipe about 4 to 6 inches in diameter can be fastened between the end plates. Use a threaded flange for fastening. You can even put holes in the pipe and bring your wiring cables through the ends.

• A four-sided wooden tube can be fashioned from lx4 or 1x6 pine or spruce, and the end plates mounted to it. Again, the cables can come through this channel and out the ends.

Notice that we've put some openings in the end plates for access -- so you can reach in and unscrew nuts from bolts or free disconnect pins.

Remember that you *have four* cable connectors at each end, one for *each* railroad module, and ONLY the selected pike's cable connector is plugged in.

The best way to handle this is to bring the module cable to a connector fixed in the L-girder end joists. That way, each module has a plug, and one cable from the end table can be plugged directly to the top module. This means *disconnecting* a module that is *not* in *use, so no* cabling problems should exist.

The challenge to the modeler is to duplicate the wiring scheme such that he has the same number of operational blocks, the same number of turnout switch machines, and that they operate in the same pattern from module to module. Otherwise, he must build different control schemes for each module.

This is an unusual and intriguing concept, certainly, but for the avid modeler - the one who likes a challenge -- we've just thrown down the gauntlet...

The Nitty-Gritty of model railroad layout planning, scenery, and wiring

As the title of this book implies, this is **The *TilTable* Book**. The text is dedicated to showing you how to build benchwork that is easier to work on and easier to modify at a later time. Certainly, *TilTable* will minimize your aches and pains since you won't be crawling under tables at the drop of a wire.

This book is *not* about layout planning, scenery, or wiring. These are each specialized subjects in model railroading, and deserve much better and more detailed treatment than can be given in this book.

There are many books written for you and your layout, scenery, and wiring problems.

Kalmbach Publishing Company has bookshelves full of titles that can keep you going for years.

Model Railroader Magazine, for instance, has articles every month on scenery and wiring, kit-bashing, scenery-structures, layouts and plans, etc.

Classic Toy Trains is another fine publication that always has something for everyone.

Books that may be of interest to you are:
101 Track Plans for Model Railroaders

How to Build Realistic Model Railroad Scenery
HO Railroad That Grows
How to Operate Your Model Railroad
Modeling the Clinchfield Railroad in N-scale
Small Railroads You Can Build
Basic Electricity and Electronics for Model Railroaders
Your Guide to Easy Model Railroad Wiring
The ABC's of Model Railroading
         And many more.

This a general sampling of the titles available to you. Check your local model railroad hobby shops, search the Internet, or write to:

Kalmbach Publishing Company, 21027 Crossroads Circle, Waukesha, WI 53187-1612

HAVE FUN
RAILROADING!

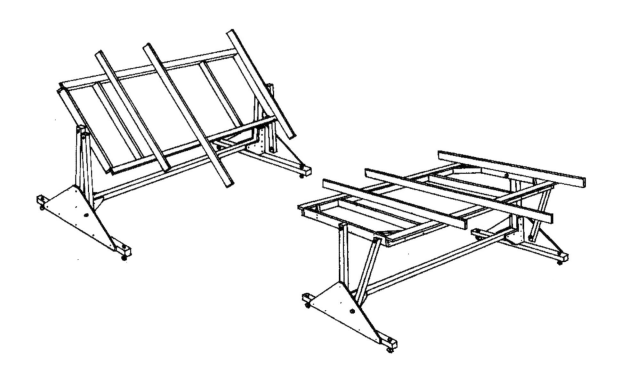

Materials List for a TILTABLE

Lumber used: Pine, Spruce, or Fir (Use lightest wood available)

No. of Parts Required	Part Name		Length	Width-in.	Thickness-in.
			1" thick solid wood parts		
2	L-girder	web	4,6, or 8 ft.	3	1
		flange	4,6, or 8 ft.	2	1
or					
2	T-girders	web	4,6, or 8 ft.	3	1
		flange	4,6, or 8 ft.	3	1
4	Girder Joists (4/table)		2,4, or 6 ft.	3	1
3,4,5	Top Joists (1 per 2 feet)		2,4, or 6 ft.	3	1
4 *	Table corner gussets (solid)		6"	6	1
			2x2 thick solid wood parts		
2	Pedestal Posts (2 per table)		40" height	2	2
2	Table Stiffeners (2 per table)		42"	2	2
or					
4	Table Stiffeners (4 per table)		42"	2	2
2	Pedestal Foot				
	(Length = Table length - 4")		44",68",92"	2	2
1	Pedestal Crossbrace		4,6, or 8 ft.	2	2
2	Diagonal crossbraces		24"	2	2
			Plywood parts -- 1/4" or 3/8" except as noted.		
2	Pedestal Gussets				
	(Length = Foot length - 8")		12" height	36",60", or 84"	
6	Diagonal Brace Gussets		6"	6"	
4	Crossbrace Gussets		15" height	6"	
4 *	Table Corner Gussets		6"	6"	3/4"
			Hardware		
4	Adjustable Feet Bolts 3/8" or 1/2" diameter				
2	Pivot Bolts 1/2" diameter				
2	Pivot Bolt Washers & Nuts 1/2"				
4 or 8	Table Stiffener Bolts (2/stiffener) 1/2" diameter x 3-1/2"				
4 or 8	Table Stiffener Bolt Washers & Nuts 1/2" diameter				
1-2 boxes	#6 x 1-1/4" Drywall Screws 100 per box				
1	Bottle of Wood Glue - medium size				

Diagram labels: TABLE JOISTS, CORNER GUSSET, W/S, W, GIRDER JOIST, L-GIRDER, PIVOT BOLT, FREE-FORM, PEDESTAL POST, CROSSBRACE GUSSET, CROSSBRACE, TABLE STIFFENER, PEDESTAL GUSSET, FOOT, ADJUSTABLE FOOT

* Table Corner Gussets may be solid wood or plywood

About the Author:

Ray Mathews is a former IBM Senior Engineer and inventor whose curiosity led him to write mysteries, thrillers, westerns, children's books in prose and verse, and non-fiction books on Finance, Bridge, Painting, Model Railroading, and others.

He and wife, Sally, have three grown children, two grandsons, and live in Raleigh, NC.

Books in print by Ray Mathews at Amazon.com include:

The Golden Crows
A Fetus Is Missing
Billy the Kid: The Hoax
8 Christmas Stories
The Book of Rhyming Stories
Bubble Ship
Growing Up and Other Stories
Tales for Boys
Nomads
Your Nest Is Your Nest Egg

E-books by Ray Mathews are at 'Smashwords.com' including all of above, plus:

How to Expand Your Painting World
The Jacoby-Stayman Bridge Bidding System
Is Self-Publishing for YOU?

Made in the USA
Charleston, SC
19 June 2013